The Digital Multinational

Management on the Cutting Edge series

Robert W. Holland Jr., series editor

Published in cooperation with *MIT Sloan Management Review*

MITSloan
Management Review

The Digital Multinational

Navigating the New Normal in Global Business

Satish Nambisan and Yadong Luo

Foreword by Conny Braams

The MIT Press
Cambridge, Massachusetts
London, England

The MIT Press would like to thank the anonymous peer reviewers who provided comments on drafts of this book. The generous work of academic experts is essential for establishing the authority and quality of our publications. We acknowledge with gratitude the contributions of these otherwise uncredited readers.

This book was set in ITC Stone Serif Std and ITC Stone Sans Std by New Best-set Typesetters Ltd. Printed and bound in the United States of America.

Library of Congress Cataloging-in-Publication Data

Names: Nambisan, Satish, author. | Luo, Yadong, author.
Title: The digital multinational : navigating the new normal in global business / Satish Nambisan and Yadong Luo; foreword by Conny Braams.
Description: Cambridge : The MIT Press, 2022. | Series: Management on the cutting edge | Includes bibliographical references and index.
Identifiers: LCCN 2021000760 | ISBN 9780262046329 (hardcover)
Subjects: LCSH: International business enterprises—Technological innovations. | Regionalism. | Globalization.
Classification: LCC HD2755.5 .N38 2022 | DDC 658/.054678—dc23
LC record available at https://lccn.loc.gov/2021000760

10 9 8 7 6 5 4 3 2 1

To Ashok, Bharat and Priya—Satish Nambisan

To Rosalie, Edward and Jady—Yadong Luo

Contents

Series Foreword

The world does not lack for management ideas. Thousands of researchers, practitioners, and other experts produce tens of thousands of articles, books, papers, posts, and podcasts each year. But only a scant few promise to truly move the needle on practice, and fewer still dare to reach into the future of what management will become. It is this rare breed of idea—meaningful to practice, grounded in evidence, and *built for the future*—that we seek to present in this series.

Robert W. Holland Jr.

Managing Director
MIT Sloan Management Review

Foreword

When Satish and Yadong invited me to write a foreword for this insightful book, my team and I had just presented Unilever's accelerated digital transformation strategy to the board. Timing is everything, or *toeval bestaat niet*, as we say in Dutch ("there is no such thing as a coincidence")! A year had passed since I had been appointed to the role of chief digital and marketing officer (CDMO), a position newly created to transform Unilever into a future-fit, purpose-led digital organization at the leading edge of marketing, serving our multistakeholder model while keeping consumers front and center.

Many have asked me whether I think it is good or bad timing that I started my role just weeks before the onset of the COVID-19 pandemic, which suddenly made everything more volatile, uncertain, ambiguous, and complex. There is a strange dichotomy in the fact that though 2020 was filled with many growing and continued hardships, which had a personalized impact on everyone, at the same time, from a professional perspective, the pace of change, the acceleration of existing trends, and the creation of new ones filled me with energy, focus, and a clear sense of direction.

After instinctively putting the safety of our people first, we then carefully considered the key trends that are likely to shape consumer priorities and behaviors in the "future normal" and, in turn, our strategies and practices to add value in the market. Two such trends are worth pointing out: the e-commerce boom and the rise of the cautious and conscious consumer. These trends did not originate due to the pandemic; rather, the pandemic accelerated what has already been happening for some time now.

With greater numbers of consumers preferring to shop online globally, e-commerce rapidly accelerated by over 60 percent year on year for Unilever. I fully expect this consumer behavior to keep growing in trend, giving rise to new market opportunities—from pure digital plays to omnichannel strategies, both requiring greater levels of innovation in product and brand offerings, not to mention higher consumer expectations for brand experiences online. We are already witnessing a surge in data-driven marketing to meet new and more personalized demands. It is also clear that the rise of e-commerce demands more operational flexibility at all levels of an organization—for example, supply chains that can accommodate smaller minimum order quantities, more frequent runs, and more bundling, or innovations needing higher value density, leading to further concentration in, say, home care products. Thus, e-commerce calls for end-to-end digital strategies that incorporate not just marketing and sales but also R&D, supply chain, analytics, and factory operations. This only strengthens the imperative to build a truly digital organization.

The second trend of a more conscious and considerate consumer increases the emphasis on the dual nature of value. In times of uncertainty, people often choose brands they trust, for both their value and their values. *Value* in terms of offering the right value equation and remaining affordable, and *values* in the sense of having a point of view that drives action on matters people truly care about. Brands are now expected to be active partners in serving both consumer and societal needs, and businesses are trusted to do so. The 2021 Edelman Trust Barometer revealed that business is the only institution deemed competent and ethical, while trust in other institutions, like governments and media, is down. It is therefore the responsibility of business to rise to the occasion and live up to the trust instilled in us by the people who buy our products.

Digital is an important part of our ability to deliver on both value and values. Digital connectivity and data analytics allow us to develop a deeper set of insights about the issues and concerns that our consumers hold as important, both globally and locally. Digital also enables us to adapt our brand and operational strategies to ensure we contribute meaningfully with solutions.

As Satish and Yadong clearly lay out in this book, concerns about income inequality, job loss, and national security in recent years have led many countries across the world to adopt protectionist measures and policies related to trade and investment. Navigating such an international business context, in which globalization and deglobalization forces coexist, can be challenging for most multinational companies. The notion of tight and loose coupling is helpful for understanding how a multinational company can organize itself digitally to accommodate both globalization and localization forces. It implies that a company's global digital connectivity with its customers, business partners, ecosystems, and operations can be calibrated to fit the unique needs of a region or market and help realize the right balance of efficiency, flexibility, and agility. One thing is for certain: the way we act upon these polarizing trends requires a big shift in multinational organizations. Digital is an important part of addressing this puzzle. It serves as the engine for rapid expansion globally while enabling more flexibility, agility, and responsiveness locally.

And though digital is an important part of the solution, I would be amiss not to point out the critical role of people, our employees, and their capabilities in achieving all this—a theme that the authors explore at length in the last chapter of this book. Equally important is the right leadership and a compass to guide the transformation. At Unilever, we act to make sustainable living commonplace based on our three beliefs: brands with purpose grow, people with purpose thrive, and companies with purpose last. These beliefs are our compass in the transformation we have embarked upon, guiding every decision for our consumers, our people, our brands, and our business. I agree with the authors' notion that senior executives who can provide a clear sense of direction and an inclusive vision for value creation—one that allows for more freedom in how such a vision is realized in practice in different regions and markets—are likely to find greater success.

The journey of transformation is an exciting adventure. I am confident that the concepts, tools, frameworks, and rich examples and case studies outlined by Satish and Yadong will act as a helpful guide to anyone embarking on this journey.

See you in the future!

Conny Braams
Chief Digital and Marketing Officer, Unilever

1 Globalization in Transition in the Digital Age

The dawn of modern globalization can be traced to the year 1000 AD.[1] That is when the Viking explorers left their homeland, crossed the North Atlantic, and reached the island of Newfoundland, connecting preexisting pan-American trade routes established by Cahokians and Mayans with those of Europe, Asia, and Africa, thereby creating new pathways that bound together different parts of the globe for the first time and facilitating movement of goods, people, and information.

Over the past thousand years or so, the nature and the contours of globalization have changed significantly, as have the key players (countries) and their motivations. And, importantly, the forces that drive globalization have also changed. The early efforts in establishing international trading posts across Asia, Africa and South America and in stitching together regional supply chains as part of the colonial economy were driven largely by advances in maritime technologies. The first industrial revolution brought about another wave of globalization facilitated by new modes of transportation (steamships, railroads), new means of production (industrial age machines), new trade routes (Suez Canal, Panama Canal), and new communication technologies (transatlantic cables). Following World War II, newer waves of globalization were launched as a result of novel institutional structures (World Trade Organization, European Union), international transport innovations (airplanes, container shipping), revolutions in manufacturing (mass production) and telecommunication technologies (satellite communication), and even managerial innovations (multidivisional structure).

Arguably, all of these forces have led to a gradual and largely predict-able advancement in both the scope and pace of globalization, par-ticularly over the last century. Indeed, starting from about the 1950s, the number of multinational enterprises (MNEs) and their global foot-prints have grown at a steady clip. For example, in the 1960s there were roughly seven thousand MNEs, but this grew to about thirty-eight thousand by the end of the millennium.

However, in the past decade or two, something unprecedented in the history of globalization has taken shape. As a 2019 World Economic Forum report noted, globalization seems to be on steroids.[2] Not only is the number of MNEs increasing exponentially (e.g., in the ten years from 2000 to 2010, the number of MNEs almost tripled to over one hun-dred thousand),[3] but MNEs also now account for half of global exports, almost one-third of world GDP, and about one-fourth of world employ-ment.[4] More importantly, many companies are now able to expand their global footprint on a pace and scale unheard of, and some are being "born global." For example, Airbnb, founded in 2008, expanded its operations into more than 191 countries in less than ten years, while Uber, launched in 2010, took only about eight years to establish a foot-print in more than sixty-three countries. OYO, an Indian hotel chain launched in 2013, has transformed into being one of the world's larg-est and fastest growing chains of leased and franchised hotels, homes, managed living, and workspaces, with presence in more than eight hundred cities in eighteen countries around the world. By contrast, Marriott International, a Maryland-based hospitality company that established its hotel business in 1957, took seventy years to expand its international footprint to about 130 countries. Similarly, it took Wyn-dham Worldwide, started in 1981, thirty years to expand its presence to around sixty-six countries, while Hilton Worldwide, started in 1919, took even more time for its global expansion to 104 countries.

What is driving this new rapid upward trajectory in globalization? The short answer is digitization.

Advances in digital technologies—from the internet and mobile computing to artificial intelligence (AI), the Internet of Things (IoT), virtual reality (VR), and blockchain—have forged new pathways to bind different parts of the world, new *information pathways*, thereby inaugurating a new era in globalization, *digital globalization*.

Digitization has allowed companies to create, deliver, and appropriate value in novel ways that are largely agnostic to national and geographical borders. Indeed, digital globalization connects international businesses and markets through flows of data, expertise, and intellectual assets and through flows of goods, services, and capital that are digitally enabled or supported. Digital technologies have also allowed more diverse sets of actors to participate in cross-border transactions than ever before, from new ventures and small businesses to multinational enterprises, enhancing the scope and reach of globalization.

And the faster-than-normal speed in global expansion is not limited to "digital natives" such as Airbnb, OYO, Uber, and Ola. Companies that deal with physical goods and services are also enjoying accelerated international expansion due to digitization. Take the case of Xiaomi, a Beijing-based handset and smartphone manufacturer. The company, which launched its flagship Mi1 line only in 2011, started its international expansion in 2014 by moving into growth markets such as Singapore, Russia, India, and Indonesia. In the few years since then, the company has rapidly expanded its global market share by expanding into more than eighty foreign markets, including Western Europe and South America (Mexico and Brazil). In India, Xiaomi is one of the more popular smartphone manufacturers, holding close to 30 percent market share.[5]

Similar experiences are evident in other established product-based companies too. For example, Philips Healthcare, a division of the Dutch conglomerate Royal Philips, accelerated its international growth, especially in emerging economies, with the launch of its HealthSuite digital health platform.[6] Similarly, multinationals such as Bayer, Johnson Controls, and John Deere have all pursued rapid digitization of their offerings and operations and enjoyed greater than normal growth in international markets.

More broadly, the convergence of digitization and globalization has created a new normal of global connectivity—one that is marked by deeper, broader, and more intricate interconnections among nations, businesses, and individuals. Digital technologies, platforms, and infrastructures are geographically unbounded, and when a company's products, services, processes, and business models are enabled by or embedded in these technologies, their portability and scalability are enhanced, making international expansion easier, cheaper, and faster. And if the globalization forces are all aligned correctly, companies can experience rapid growth in their global footprints. For example, Airbnb's digital platform (and accompanying business model) is highly portable across national and regional boundaries, enabling the company to "copy and paste" its digital global strategy and operations into remote corners of the world. At the same time, globalization has led to an exploding global tourism industry, especially in emerging economies in Asia, Africa, and Latin America, which has driven up the demand for the company's offerings. While the COVID-19 pandemic has acted as a damper for international travel and tourism, in the longer term, according to the World Travel & Tourism Council (WTTC), travel to emerging economies is expected to increase at twice the rate of travel to advanced economies, a growth that companies such as OYO and Airbnb are well positioned to exploit.

Yet the promise of such digital globalization is increasingly being hampered by the emergence of an alternative narrative of deglobalization—*localization and geopolitical nationalism*.

It is true that over its thousand or so years of history, globalization has waxed and waned, driven by a host of factors—from wars and conquests to pandemics and trade disputes between nations. For example, World War I led to the collapse of interbank cooperation and expansion of controls on trade, migration, and agriculture and effectively put an end to the international economy led by Great Britain. The resulting deglobalization was further accentuated by the Great Depression in the 1930s and led to a significant collapse in international trade and capital flows.

In recent years, however, concerns about income inequality, job loss, dislocation, national security, and illegal immigration have shifted the conversation about global trade and investment away from a focus on economic benefits and toward more protectionism. This shift is remarkable in two respects. First, unlike in the 1930s, when deglobalization decisions were largely driven by autocracies, this time they seem to have originated in democracies across the world.[7] For example, several nations, including prior champions of free trade such as the United States and the United Kingdom, have adopted tit-for-tat tariff escalation moves and enacted policies to restrict foreign corporate mergers, immigration, and international data transfers. Similar protectionist measures have also taken hold in the largest democracy in the world, India. While some of these policies may go away with changes in governments, the broader protectionist trend is unlikely to disappear until the underlying causes also go away. For example, as US Federal Reserve Chair Jerome Powell noted in late 2020, while technological advances are going to be positive for societies in the long term, in the short to medium term the pains due to such forces are likely to affect certain parts of the society more, increasing income inequalities and sustaining the reasons for protectionist measures the world over.[8]

Second, digitization itself has become a factor driving some of these deglobalization decisions as concerns about digital colonialism and digital sovereignty assume center stage in many parts of the world. For example, within the EU, there are serious concerns that non-EU-based companies such as Google and Amazon may come to dominate entire sectors of the EU economy, depriving member states of their sovereignty in areas such as data protection and taxation. Similarly, the growing reliance on digital infrastructures and equipment from non-EU-based companies—such as the Chinese 5G infrastructure—has raised critical cybersecurity and national security concerns.[9] If data is indeed the new oil, then there is no doubt that the continued absence of effective worldwide regulations will lead to more such concerns and the ensuing protectionist measures across the world.

This negative geopolitical narrative of growing protectionism is reflected in globalization metrics that indicate slowdown in global trade, capital flow, and foreign direct investment (FDI). As per the 2018

DHL Global Connectedness Index report, if the world had really become "flat" and such trade constraints no longer mattered, international trade, capital, information, and people flows would be expected to travel 67 percent further than they do today—thus providing tangible, data-based support for the impact of the new geopolitical reality of regionalization and localization.[10] Such localization and nationalism that has taken root in many parts of the world, including parts of Asia, Europe, Africa, and South America, presents new and complex challenges for multinational companies as they ponder their next international business expansion moves.

Importantly, the COVID-19 pandemic has severely impacted both of these narratives—both digital globalization and deglobalization/localization. On the one hand, a key outcome of the pandemic has been a transformative growth in the adoption or use of digital technologies the world over. For example, it has been estimated that consumer and business digital technology adoption vaulted five years forward in a matter of around eight weeks.[11] From "lights-out factories" (fully automated, hands-off operations) and remote sales to remote work (working from home), telemedicine, and online education, digital technologies have penetrated the creation, delivery, and consumption of value in all types of industries. This is evident in all parts of the world and across all segments of the population. Consider the following statistic. In the US, it took a decade (from 2009 to 2019) for e-commerce penetration (by percentage of retail sales) to increase more than ten percentage points from 5.6 percent to 16 percent. However, the next ten-percentage-point increase took less than eight weeks: it grew to 27 percent by the end of April 2020.[12] Similarly, in India, the use of digital apps and smartphones by smallholder farmers surged so much during the COVID-19 quarantine period (April to May 2020) that the growth in adoption that was expected to happen in two to three years occurred in a month or so.[13] Indeed, the profound impact of such an exponential pace of digitization experienced by the global economy may force future business historians to study globalization in terms of two different eras: BC (before COVID-19) and AC (after COVID-19).[14]

On the other hand, the COVID-19 pandemic has acted as an accelerant to the nationalistic and protective tendencies ascendant across the world. New barriers to the movement of goods and people across countries have come into existence, further exacerbating deglobalization efforts. There are increasing calls for "economic self-reliance" and "strategic autonomy" in several parts of the world, including India, China, Japan, and the EU. For example, Japan's COVID-19 stimulus includes subsidies for firms that repatriate factories. As per the 2020 World Investment Report, more than seventy countries have taken measures to shield their domestic industries from foreign takeovers, and the pandemic could have lasting effects on globalization in terms of a "shift towards more restrictive admission policies for foreign investment in strategic industries."[15] All of this has raised important questions related to the pandemic's effect on international business, even provoking magazine article titles such as "Has COVID-19 Killed Globalization?"[16]

Thus, while *digitization* in general promotes greater levels of interconnectedness among businesses (and nations), enhancing the extent of globalization, *localization and geopolitical nationalism* pose important barriers to such interconnectedness, limiting the extent of globalization. It is this contrasting set of scenarios—the unfettered global economy promised by digital globalization and the barrier-bound global economy marked by localization and nationalism—that has created the *new normal* for international business, one that presents complex challenges for multinational companies.

Indeed, as Uber and other multinationals have realized, they can no longer port their business by simply copying and pasting their digital global business strategy into different parts of the world. A careful examination of Uber's experience in some of the Asian markets indicates that while its digital platform (and associated infrastructure) enabled the company to enjoy network effects and fast entry into new foreign markets, the company failed to adequately read and adapt its strategy to the prevailing geopolitical realities, including regulatory barriers, conflicting labor laws and institutional practices, and conditions favoring home-grown competitors such as Ola.

In such instances, Uber—or, for that matter, any multinational—will be required to adapt their digital global business strategies to fit the realities of the particular foreign market. But how should companies reenvision their digital global business strategies? More broadly, how should companies devise and deploy digital global business strategies that reflect the promise held out by digitization and yet (acknowledge and) adapt to the peculiarities and the geopolitical realities of the regions and nations in which they will be practiced?

It is this question that motivated us to write this book.

In the remainder of this chapter, we first tease out the key differences in global businesses between the twentieth and twenty-first centuries and then discuss the need for multinationals to build their *digital global business connectivity* as the anchor for their global expansion initiatives.

Differences in Global Business between the Twentieth Century and the Twenty-First Century

A careful examination of the differences in global business between the current and the last century helps to highlight the parameters of the changes wrought by digital globalization and regionalization/localization and the ensuing challenges and opportunities for companies as they pursue global expansion.

Dominance of Intangible Flows of Information and Digital Infrastructures

Flows of physical goods and finance were the hallmarks of the twentieth-century global economy, but today those flows have flattened or declined. Global business in the twenty-first century is increasingly defined by flows of data, information, and knowledge. Indeed, cross-border data flows have grown over fifty times larger between 2005 and 2019 as digital flows of commerce, information, video, and intracompany traffic continue to surge, far more so than global flows of trade and finance.[17] Digital connectivity changes the economics of doing business across borders, bringing down the cost of international interactions and transactions.

This is also reflected in the increasing significance of digital infrastructures. While physical infrastructure conditions, such as transportation, real estate, communications, and utilities, were the key determinants for foreign market location selection in the past century, digital infrastructure has become equally if not more important for international businesses in the twenty-first century. For instance, easy access to and availability of cloud-based computing infrastructure critically affects a company's ability to rapidly scale its operations in a foreign market and to consistently deliver a new class of experience-focused services worldwide.

A Remarkable Rise in the Number of Micromultinationals

Globalization was once driven principally by large multinational enterprises (and major financial institutions and powerful governments). Today, a large number of new ventures and small businesses have assumed an active role in globalization, especially through their participation in digital e-commerce platforms with global reach. For example, small businesses worldwide are becoming *micromultinationals* by using digital platforms such as eBay, Amazon, and Alibaba to connect with customers and suppliers in other countries. Amazon now hosts some two million third-party sellers, many of whom are primarily exporters. Indeed, small businesses account for about 48 percent of India's exports, indicating the outsized role such companies play in the international business emanating from emerging economies. Many digital start-ups are *born global enterprises*; they use the "plug-and-play" infrastructure of digital platforms to put themselves in front of an enormous base of global customers. For example, China's DJI is a born-global venture. From its inception in 2006 in Shenzhen, the company targeted international markets, benefiting from direct access to global suppliers and consumers through digital platforms. It is the world's largest manufacturer of drones for commercial and consumer use today, holding over 70 percent of global market share.

A Huge Shift in Consumer Power in Shaping Global Business

Thanks to social media and other digital platforms, individuals and consumers are forming their own cross-border connections and shaping global business to a much greater extent. By 2020, there were close to four billion social media users across the world, and an increasing proportion of these (about 20 percent) took part in cross-border e-commerce.[18] As social media exposes consumers from around the world to what is available, products can go viral on a scale never seen before. Digital platforms also offer individuals new ways to learn from, collaborate with, and influence peer consumers. For example, digital platforms such as TikTok have given rise to a new generation of consumer influencers who can expand the global reach of companies and drive brand adoption across the world, often assuming greater power than the companies' own internal marketing departments. Importantly, global consumers also influence companies' decisions and operations directly through online feedback and reviews.

Increased Participation, Contribution, and Influence of Emerging Economies

In the predigital world, developing countries, particularly emerging economies, used to be weak players in global business, but today they are powerhouses for the global economy. Emerging economies are counterparts in more than half of global trade flows, and South-South trade is the fastest-growing type of connection. These emerging markets are going through simultaneous industrial and urban revolutions, as well as institutional changes, shifting the center of the world economy more toward major emerging economies. For example, nearly half of global GDP growth between 2010 and 2025 is expected to come from 440 cities in emerging markets—95 percent of them small and medium-sized cities.[19] This has prompted many multinationals to shift their traditional top-down approach (which treats emerging markets as mere implementers of global initiatives) to a more bottom-up approach (which involves building global initiatives around emerging markets). As a consequence, there is growing trend for multinationals to choose large, vibrant cities in emerging markets as their regional or even global headquarters, select successful business models from emerging markets to be applied globally, and designate emerging market subsidiaries as global innovators or strategic leaders for their global operations—all of which indicate the significance of the emerging economies in international business.

Increasing Prevalence of Global Business Ecosystems

Global business ecosystems have increasingly become the primary vehicle for multinationals to interact, cooperate, and share a set of dependencies with other companies across the world in the process of producing and delivering products, technologies, and services for global customers. In addition to suppliers, distributors, manufacturers, technology providers, and system integrators, such business ecosystems also include customers, finance providers (e.g., venture capitalists, corporate investors, investment banks, angel investors), universities and research institutions, regulatory authorities, industry standard-setting bodies, and the like. One central force spurring the growth of global business ecosystems is digital connectivity. During the last two decades, the business infrastructure has become much more digital, with increased interconnections among products, processes, technologies, and services. And this in turn has led to more open global ecosystems that allow for flexibility and scalability in interfirm relationships across industries/sectors and countries.

These digitally enabled business ecosystems also leverage the openness of the global market for acquiring intermediary resources or services (such as professional industrial design services, total logistics solutions, and advertising and promotion services). The rapid infusion of digital technologies, increased modularity, and standardization of these intermediary services across countries encourages companies to adopt more flexible and open global business models. As *New York Times* columnist Thomas Friedman noted, "Accelerations in digitization and globalization are steadily making more work modular," rendering companies as platforms "that synthesize and orchestrate these modular packets to make products and services."[20] Cross-sharing of such key modular resources, including distribution channels and supply bases, among companies within an industry or even among those in different industries is unprecedentedly prevalent due to heightened needs for quick market responses, sophisticated global demands, and synergetic gains from complementary cooperation.

Mutual Flows of Knowledge and Innovation between Advanced and Emerging Economies

In the twentieth century, innovation and knowledge were largely transferred from developed countries to developing countries. But in the twenty-first century, these flows (including technologies, product ideas, and even business models) go in both directions. For example, a centuries-old homeopathic honey-based remedy for coughs and cold became the source for Vicks Cough Syrup with Honey from Procter & Gamble (P&G). This product was first developed for lower-income consumers in Mexico and Brazil and then marketed to consumers in Europe and the United States. Many international companies have undertaken such "reverse innovation" initiatives—wherein an innovation is developed and adopted first in a developing/emerging economy and then marketed to the rest of the world, including developed countries.[21] This has also led multinationals to adopt the practice of transforming local talent to global talent as an essential component of their global knowledge and innovation strategy. For example, the largest multidisciplinary integrated R&D center at General Electric (GE), the John F. Welch Technology Centre, is located in Bengaluru, India, and employs more than five thousand engineers and scientists. Similarly, Goldman Sachs's Bengaluru office, which serves as a global in-house center with more than three thousand engineers, has emerged as a key innovation hub for the company and has played an instrumental role in the development of Marcus, its new digital consumer banking platform. These subsidiaries are increasingly playing a global innovator rule, serving as the fountainhead of knowledge not just for the focal host country but for the multinationals' overall global market. As Harit Talwar, the chairman of Goldman Sachs's consumer business noted, "When multinational companies have voracious appetite for talent, they have to be in all those places where such talent is located"—and these days, that increasingly includes the emerging economies.[22]

Weakened Multilateral Governance and Escalated Geopolitical Volatility

In the twentieth century, globalization, especially trade, had been principally governed by strong multilateral treaties or organizations that set forth and overhauled trade policy rules. These rules aimed to foster nondiscrimination, transparency, and predictability in the conduct of international trade. The World Trade Organization (WTO), for instance, pursues such objectives by administering trade agreements, acting as a forum for trade negotiations, settling trade disputes, reviewing national trade policies, assisting developing countries on trade policy issues, and cooperating with other international organizations. But the WTO is weakened in the twenty-first century. It failed to produce adequate or notable progress on many fronts in recent years. The failure of the WTO as a negotiating forum has limited the extent to which its rules address modern trade concerns and has put pressure on the dispute settlement system.

Along with weakened multilateral governance (organizations and treaties), global geopolitics has become profusely complex, volatile, and fragile in the new century. Globalization has always produced winners and losers, even at its inception in 1000 AD.[23] But the dark side of globalization has become more acute today, in part due to the ineffectiveness of the governing systems of world economic and geopolitical order. As nationalism and protectionism grow in many countries, international companies, regardless of their origin, size, and sector, encounter greater uncertainty and unpredictability today than ever before. For example, data sovereignty concerns have led many countries to seek control of the internet within the jurisdictional boundaries of the nation-states (network-state alignment), putting multinationals at the mercy of potentially erratic political decision-making.[24] China is a case in point: it has long advocated for the concept of "cyber sovereignty" (*wangluo zhuquan*) to exercise localized control of the internet and data flows, as well as, more recently, digital currency.[25]

What International Businesses Gain and Risk via Digitization and Localization

All of the changes mentioned thus far that have emerged in the global business context in recent years translate into a set of new opportunities and challenges for international businesses, both nascent and established. Before we consider how companies should adapt their digital global business strategies to successfully navigate the globalization and localization forces, it would be useful to look at what there is to gain and to risk from doing so. We can identify three broad sets of benefits or gains from digitization forces.

First, there is a *global customer effect*. Digitization massively enlarges the pool of customers, consumers, and end users all over the world and, importantly, makes it readily accessible to international business (even small businesses) in a cost-effective manner. Digital platforms and e-commerce marketplaces such as Alibaba, Amazon, Pinduoduo, eBay, Flipkart, and Rakuten provide a huge built-in base of potential customers and effective ways to market to those customers directly and launch new products. With global retail e-commerce traffic going up drastically due to the COVID-19 crisis, these digital marketplaces have gained outsized significance.[26] Further, social media and other such digital platforms enable small and medium-sized international enterprises to engage with these global customers in ways that are both intimate and economical. In the fashion industry, for example, bloggers, vloggers, Instagrammers, and Twitter users are accelerating trends by highlighting what celebrities wear and then following that up with an appropriate set of offerings to global markets.

Second, there is a *transaction cost effect*. Digitization significantly reduces cross-border transaction costs for international companies. By reducing the cost of transactions and allowing digital goods, services, and capital to change hands instantly, digitization is creating a more hyperconnected, hyperspeed era of global flows. Exporting, for instance, is not merely much easier but also significantly cheaper and faster than ever before due to digital connectivity. This connectivity also nurtures a large number of export or logistics service providers in different countries who furnish, in very cost-efficient ways and in real time, total services (or solutions), including international logistics and other export services, for small businesses.

Third, there is an *open innovation effect*. Digitization bolsters the innovativeness and creativity of international companies as it allows them to connect with talent, seek out novel ideas in different countries, and develop those ideas into new products, services, and business models that can be deployed in other foreign markets in seamless ways. Global open ecosystems that international companies establish can encompass an entire universe of diverse participants, including foreign suppliers, industrial designers and service providers, global distributors, foreign manufacturers, foreign universities, R&D hubs in different regions, country and regional headquarters, and, importantly, customers worldwide.

Finally, there is a *managerial efficiency effect*. Digitization augments international companies' capabilities and effectiveness in planning, organizing, and monitoring globally dispersed activities and operations. A whole host of enterprise-level digital platforms and solutions—from cloud computing, 5G, and 3D printing to blockchain, IoT, and AI/analytics—has made it possible for an international company to diversify and scale its operations worldwide and at the same time maintain its visibility into its operations in remote parts of the world. Importantly, such digitization also helps remove barriers due to organizational boundaries and enable operational visibility across the value network. Digital connectivity may take on a deeper dimension in the near future as more companies embed monitors, sensors, and tracking devices into their physical assets, thus enabling them to find more efficient and effective ways to organize and manage global resources and operations.

While recognizing these opportunities stemming from rapid digitization, we cannot underrate the following three types of risks and challenges that follow from the increasing levels of regionalization/localization.

First, there is a *complexity risk*. Globalization and localization forces enhance the overall complexity of operations as a greater number of locations, partners, and other entities are added to the multinationals' portfolios with widely varying roles, capabilities, goals and priorities. Managing large intra- and interfirm networks across national, cultural, economic, and institutional boundaries is a daunting undertaking, despite the connectivity that digital technologies afford. Without superior relational and orchestration capabilities, companies are likely to suffer from risks related to both inefficient value creation and inadequate value appropriation.

Second, there are *contagion risks*. As companies expand into foreign markets, they become dependent on their foreign partners to varied extents and thus subject to contagious effects from all the risks that ensue from globalization and localization forces (including social unrest, political instability, and natural disasters). For example, the risks emanating from the recent trade disputes between the US and China have gradually diffused into a number of companies and industries, including some not directly tied to the focal areas of dispute. Similarly, the supply chain disruptions caused by the COVID-19 pandemic affected entire business ecosystems, halting the operations of big and small companies alike. The impact of such external shocks is magnified in a more interconnected world, and ripple effects spread even faster in a digitized world. Such contagion effects can also include data privacy, cybersecurity, intellectual property (IP) theft, and reputational risks, related to both a multinational and its global partners. For example, the ripple effects from a cybersecurity breach at a partner firm in one country can easily travel across the multinational's network and affect partners in other countries.

Third, there is a *competition risk*. While digital globalization has enabled multinationals to expand their global footprint faster and cheaper, localization has fostered the emergence and growth of a large number of new types of global rivals: local companies that take advantage of favorable (or protectionist) local and regional conditions. Despite their smallness or newness, these new global players are fast and agile, often adopting new, digital connectivity–enabled business models that allow them to rapidly appropriate new, "fitted" customer value propositions in diverse regional contexts (e.g., consider the expansion of Indian ride-hailing company Ola into other Asian markets, such as Singapore, and more recently into the UK, Australia, and New Zealand). Thus, the very same digital infrastructure that has enabled entry into foreign markets has also led to crowded competition in specific regional and national markets (such as India, China, and Brazil), enhancing the associated risks for foreign multinationals.

These benefits and risks imply the need for international companies to acquire or build an appropriate set of capabilities to navigate the increasingly dynamic and complex digital global business landscape. In the remainder of this book, our aim is to present a set of ideas and practices that would enable companies to address these challenges and enhance their success in international business expansion and growth.

Global Business Strategies for the Digital Age

Our discussion so far illustrates the need for companies to navigate a global business landscape that is increasingly characterized by both globalization and deglobalization, or localization, forces. It is also evident from our examples that digital technologies will form a critical element of a company's global business strategy as it pursues international expansion in such a challenging landscape. By *digital global business strategies*, we mean global business strategies that are enabled by or built on unique digital technology-based capabilities. Such digital global business strategies can involve identifying and pursuing new foreign market opportunities, engaging with foreign customers, collaborating with foreign partners to deploy or augment a company's firm-specific advantages or assets, innovating in offerings and business models, and/ or coordinating operations across different internal units located in multiple foreign countries.

Our primary thesis in this book is that companies can devise and deploy appropriate digital global business strategies to navigate both globalized and localized business landscapes. Specifically, we explain the paradoxical role of digital technologies in the global business context: while digital technologies can serve as the engine for rapid business expansion in a globalized context by enhancing the portability and scalability of a company's business model and internal assets, the same set of digital technologies can also help the company to become more flexible and responsive to the peculiarities of a localized context. To describe the set of digital global business strategies that would underlie such a paradoxical role, we introduce the concept of digital global business connectivity.

We define *digital global business connectivity* as a company's connectivity along four key dimensions of its business that are enabled by or founded on digital technologies: with global customers and markets, with global partners and ecosystems, with global resources and knowledge, and with operations and activities distributed across the world. The four dimensions represent a holistic view of a multinational's global value creation—for whom (customers and markets), where (partners/ecosystems and operations/activities), and how (resources and knowledge). Thus, digital global business connectivity forms a critical *business capability* that is derived from the company's digitally enabled conduits of information, influence, and action with regard to its far-flung set of customers and markets, partners and ecosystems, resources and knowledge, and operations and activities.[27]

The significance of digital global business connectivity was evidenced in a survey of multinationals that we conducted (see figure 1.1).[28] Almost 84 percent of the respondents marked digital global business connectivity as high or very high in importance for their company. At the same time, only a minority of respondents (approximately 23 percent) agreed that their company was well prepared or equipped to achieve digital global business connectivity. The disparity in the two sets of ratings indicates the gap in the understanding of the strategies and practices needed to achieve digital global business connectivity and, in turn, motivates our book.

Importantly, digital global business connectivity implies a balance between responsiveness and distinctiveness; *responsiveness* ensures that the different subsidiaries, partners, or parts of the multinational can operate together or are responsive to one another, whereas *distinctiveness* ensures that individual subsidiaries and partners adapt to and reflect the distinctive aspects of the local context. As we discuss in more detail in the next chapter, responsiveness without distinctiveness relates to *tight*

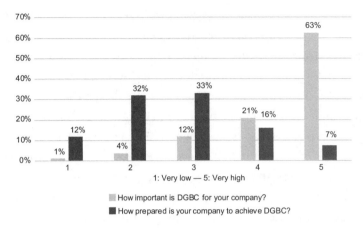

Figure 1.1

Significance of digital global business connectivity (DGBC)—survey findings

coupling, whereas responsiveness and distinctiveness together relate to *loose coupling*.[29] Thus, digital global business connectivity is reflected in the governance choices a company makes with regard to the extent of tightness or looseness in its relationships along each of the four key dimensions.

For example, in more globalized business landscapes, digital technologies can help infuse more tightness into a firm's business relationships/interactions and operations by emphasizing rapid and more efficient deployment of firm-specific advantages and assets. Consider the initiative by Moog, a $2.9 billion aircraft component maker, to combine blockchain and 3D printing technologies. This allows it to speed up the replacement of defective aircraft parts anywhere in the world, from multiple weeks to a few hours. The company uses its blockchain system (VeriPart) to allow its global customers (airline companies) to place orders for aircraft parts, to acquire design files from partner firms, and to validate their orders and create the paper trails required by different national regulatory agencies such as the FAA. It then transmits each order to one of its global facilities, where the replacement part is printed using the company's 3D printer. In a recent demonstration of this level of responsiveness, one Moog customer, Air New Zealand, ordered a part (an in-seat screen for a Boeing 777-300) while the flight was en route from Auckland to Los Angeles. The company sourced the design file from a partner, Singapore Technologies Engineering, and transmitted that to its Los Angeles facility, where it was printed and delivered to the airline by the time the flight landed there.

Such digitally enabled global responsiveness may not be sufficient in localized business landscapes, where the ability to demonstrate distinctiveness may be equally or more critical. Where localization and nationalistic forces are ascendant, digital technologies can help infuse more looseness in a firm's relationships and interactions, allowing for more latitude in fitting the firm's assets, offerings, business models, policies, and operations to particular regional/local conditions. To give a simple example, one of the factors behind the early success of India-based ride-sharing company Ola has been its ability to establish relationships with a wide range of payment systems in different geographic locations (from cash and credit/debit cards to private digital wallet service providers such as JioMoney in India and Apple Pay in Australia and New Zealand), thereby allowing for more flexibility in its business model to cater to regional customers.

As we describe in this book, companies need to adopt a portfolio of digital global business strategies that incorporates *tight* digital global business connectivity in some aspects of their business and *loose* digital global business connectivity in some other aspects. The challenge for senior multinational executives then is to decide on the appropriate portfolio of digital global business strategies for their company based on the specific foreign markets and businesses it operates in globally. Obviously, this would require managers to analyze the conditions that are present in different geographical markets, evaluate the need for tightness and looseness in their digital global business connectivity, and then put together a coherent set of strategies.

In this book, our goal is to guide the reader in this decision-making process by identifying the parameters that shape the tightness-looseness requirements of digital global business connectivity (chapter 2), describing how these requirements lead to different digital global business strategies related to the four dimensions of digital global business connectivity (chapters 3–6) and then explaining how these different strategies can be put together as a coherent portfolio, taking into consideration the associated risks and requisite capabilities (chapters 7–10). Figure 1.2 depicts the broad framework that will guide this book.

Now, let's briefly describe the layout of the remaining chapters. In chapter 2, we describe in detail the concept of tight and loose coupling and describe how such a framing can help companies develop a deeper understanding of the digital global business connectivity they will need

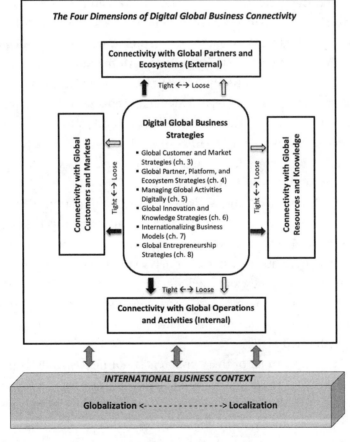

Figure 1.2
Global business strategies for the digital age

in the emerging global business context. As noted previously, forces due to digitization and localization shape the landscape for digital global business connectivity. Based on the intensity of these two forces—that is, digital forces and regional/local forces—we develop a typology of global business contexts. We then use this typology to describe how the tightness and looseness of digital global business connectivity may vary across different contexts.

Following that (in chapters 3–6), we consider the set of digital global business strategies that can help companies achieve digital global business connectivity in terms of each of the four dimensions. Chapter 3 focuses on the dimension of global customers and markets and incorporates digital strategies related to entering new foreign markets and engaging with global customers. In chapter 4, we discuss strategies for establishing and orchestrating digital platforms and ecosystems and creating new opportunities for collaboration and value cocreation with global partners. Chapter 5 relates to digitally enabled strategies for organizing and managing globally dispersed activities, including managing foreign subsidiaries. In chapter 6, we discuss new digitally enabled approaches to acquire knowledge and other resources and to pursue innovation in the global arena.

Next (in chapters 7 and 8), we consider two important contexts in which the sets of strategies from chapters 3–6 come together. Specifically, chapter 7 relates to strategies for internationalizing and creating novel digitally enabled business models to fit different foreign markets. And in chapter 8, we examine strategies related to different types of digitally enabled international entrepreneurship—from micro-MNEs and digital-born globals to international corporate entrepreneurship from established MNEs.

Our objective in all of these chapters is not merely to describe a set of strategies but to show how companies can bring together appropriate sets of digital technologies and enterprise capabilities in ways that take into consideration the prevailing globalization-localization context and achieve the right levels of tightness and looseness in digital global business connectivity. As such, while we use examples from international companies from across the world to illustrate these strategies, we also clarify the international business context—in terms of government regulations/policies, business/digital infrastructure, and business/consumer culture—to underline its relevance.

It is important to pause and restate one thing here. Digital global business connectivity is not a technological connectivity or capability. It is a *business capability*.

Certainly, it relies on a host of powerful digital technologies, platforms and infrastructure—from social media, mobile and wearable computing, blockchain, virtual and augmented reality (VR and AR), and cloud computing to AI, robotics, IoT, digital sensors, and 3D printing. But these and other digital technologies in and by themselves are not sufficient; we need digital global business strategies that marry those technologies with other firm-level complementary capabilities and assets to realize a multinational's digital global business connectivity. And our focus in this book is on these digital global business strategies.

Our objective in the final two chapters (chapters 9 and 10) is to pull all these ideas together and provide a concise template and toolkit for managers to evaluate and make decisions using the notion of digital global business connectivity. To this end, in chapter 9, we expand on the many risks that digital global business connectivity entails. We identify the nature and sources of these risks (both digital and nondigital), provide a scale to evaluate the risks, and discuss strategies and practices that multinationals can adopt to manage them. We conclude the book in chapter 10 by describing some of the key digital capabilities—from digital intelligence to digital resilience—needed for the successful execution of the strategies associated with digital global business connectivity. In effect, in the last chapter, we answer the question: Now that I know about the potential opportunities and strategies related to digital global business connectivity, how exactly should I proceed to put some of these ideas into practice at my company?

The Key Takeaways for the Reader

We wrote this book for two primary audiences.

The first is a CEO or senior business executive who has the primary responsibility for driving the international growth of a business unit or a major business corporation. For you, we provide a broad understanding of how companies can achieve international growth through digital global business connectivity, as well as a roadmap for developing such connectivity in your company. Notably, we situate our ideas in the post-COVID-19 new normal of global business, one characterized by the pushes and pulls from forces due to digitization and localization. As such, the ideas offered here are not meant to be pie-in-the-sky concepts; rather, we offer a realistic set of digital global business strategies and practices, as well as a clear articulation of the associated rewards and risks, so that you can make informed decisions about your company's future, digitally fueled, global expansion initiatives.

The second audience for the book is (a) a manager, in a large or midsized corporation, tasked with leading global business development initiatives; and (b) an entrepreneur of a small or medium-sized enterprise who is trying to internationalize and expand a young venture. For you, we bring clarity to the aspects of digital global business strategies that you should pay attention to in your company's unique context: the digital technologies and organizational capabilities that you will need to invest in, the risks you will need to manage, and the outcomes you can expect. More broadly, we offer a detailed roadmap for you to proceed with your company's global initiatives in a measured manner.

Allow us to clarify an important thing. We picked the title for this book, *The Digital Multinational*, quite intentionally. By "digital multinational," we do not mean to refer to only the Airbnbs and Ubers of this world—that is, multinationals that are digital natives. Rather, with digitization seeping into varied aspects of multinationals' international operations and offerings, *all* multinational enterprises are becoming digital multinationals. As Conny Braams noted in her foreword, Unilever is aiming to become "a future-fit, purpose-led digital organization."

Indeed, it is not just Unilever. All the multinationals whose stories we narrate in this book—from consumer product multinationals such as Burberry and Lululemon to industrial product multinationals such as Bayer, Johnson Controls, and Aditya Birla Group—are evolving into digital multinationals in some form or other. As such, the insights from this book apply to all types of multinationals—digital natives as well as non-natives.

What industries or markets is this book particularly relevant for? The notion of digital global business connectivity and related business strategies apply equally well to a broad array of industries in which the pace of digitization has accelerated in recent years. This includes firms that cater to consumer markets, both the packaged goods consumer sector (e.g., food, personal products, fashion, consumer electronics, home appliances) and the service sector (e.g., entertainment, banking). It is also relevant to other industries or fields, such as automotive, retail, health, and agriculture, in which digitization has revolutionized business models and offerings. Importantly, as our numerous examples illustrate, these ideas can be applied whether you are expanding your business into developed or emerging economies. In addition, the essential concepts behind digital global business connectivity can be applied in the nonprofit world, too, as nonprofits of all stripes are trying to expand their boundaries in search of new customers, partners, and resources.

Now, join us as we begin this journey by exploring the novel concept of digital global business connectivity.

2 Digital Global Business Connectivity

In the last chapter, we mentioned that the forces of digitization and localization may vary across different international markets, even within an industry. The global auto industry is illustrative of this. In 2018, Indonesia (and a few other countries in Southeast Asia) adopted a set of protectionist measures to limit car imports and to promote more local auto production, including additional certification requirements for foreign companies and tax incentives for local manufacturers.[1] Further, while the country has recently embarked on an ambitious digital initiative, its auto sector has lagged behind that of most other countries in its digitization capabilities. Its next-door neighbor, Malaysia, which has a much longer history of auto manufacturing, is more digitized but susceptible to a similar set of localization forces. Compared to that, the EU presents a different scenario—one characterized by higher levels of digitization and lower levels of localization. Right next door, the UK's auto industry, while highly digitized, is marked by strong Brexit localization forces.

Understanding the nature and structure of such variations in international markets is a must for multinationals to succeed. To this end, in this chapter, we develop a typology of global business contexts based on the intensity of digital and regional/local forces, and we identify the two contexts for establishing digital global business connectivity: digital globalization and digital localization.

Intensity of Digital Forces

Digital forces are ascendant across most industries and sectors. For instance, digital components are now evident in a wide range of products that we use on a daily basis—from smart home appliances to smart shoes and apparel. Our automobiles have become smart devices on wheels. Increasingly, these digitally embedded products are part of a broader ecosystem of offerings that operate on digital platforms (e.g., Google's Nest Weave, Ford's SYNC, Johnson Controls' OpenBlue, Herman Miller Live, or MyJohnDeere). Digital technologies are also reshaping companies' internal operations, including global manufacturing and supply chain processes. The set of digital technologies collectively referred to as the fourth industrial revolution (4IR)—including advanced robotics, 3D printing, AI, IoT, blockchain, augmented reality, and virtual reality—has reshaped entire global value chains, from production planning and manufacturing to logistics and distribution. The number of IoT devices is projected to surpass forty-one billion and generate 79.4 zettabytes (ZB) of data by 2025, implying the extent to which such sensors and the associated data will drive global commerce.[2] Similarly, the fusion of 5G, AI, and IoT—termed *intelligent connectivity*—is expected to deliver personalized experiences to users in a host of industries, including retail, health, and entertainment.

Digital technologies possess several important characteristics that render this business transformation unique, and two characteristics in particular are worth mentioning in the context of global business.

First, digital technologies are *country (or location) agnostic*, in that they can be made available (and used) across national borders with limited additional effort; that is, they exhibit a *distributedness* characteristic.[3] This allows for companies to market their digitally enabled products and services globally with ease; their use is no longer limited to or confined by geographical and institutional boundaries and instead is dependent only on access to appropriate digital infrastructures.

Second, digital technologies and components are *generative* in nature in that they can be easily modified and combined with other technologies—even by entities other than those that created them in the first place—to deliver newer sets of services and capabilities. Such technology generativity, which arises from their openness and recombinability, allows for rapidly refashioning the value proposition of a product/service (or business model) to fit localized needs.[4] For example, over the years, numerous new services tailored to different global market needs have been developed by digital entrepreneurs across the world by combining/modifying the Google Maps platform with other digital assets—from providing turn-by-turn navigation in countries not supported by Google to customizing the native language/voice for delivery of turn-by-turn directions.

At the same time, technology generativity leads to consequences that are not always linear; that is, it renders the trajectory of evolution of products/services and business models unpredictable to certain extent. For instance, the actions of third-party app developers on consumer-facing (Google Android) and industry-facing (ThingWorx industrial IoT) digital platforms are often unpredictable and can lead to new pathways of value creation not originally envisioned by platform owners. As we discuss in later chapters, these two characteristics have enormous consequences for how companies pursue global expansion of their businesses.

While digitization is prevalent in most industries, the intensity of digital forces varies across industries. Consider the management of power, water, and other natural resources. In the past decade or so, digitally enabled smart systems have become operational in many of these areas, allowing for more efficient asset management and distribution. For example, digitally enabled "connected utility" systems have allowed water companies to seamlessly integrate informational and operational technologies (including digital sensors and algorithm-driven analytics) to improve water extraction through smart pumps and/or treatment through real-time performance monitoring.[5] But when compared with the automotive sector, the utilities industry clearly lags behind in both the diversity and the intensity of digital transformation. For example, in the automotive industry, connected cars and digitized ecosystems have reshaped entire global value chains (as well as processes), bringing in nontraditional partners (media companies, software start-ups) and their diverse value offerings. Indeed, the global connected car market is expected to grow fivefold from $42 billion in 2019 to about $212 billion by 2027, reflecting the extent of industry growth driven by digitization.[6]

Importantly, the intensity of digital forces within an industry may also vary across geographical regions or markets. As Shiv Shivakumar, group executive president at India's Aditya Birla Group, rightly pointed out, "It is not enough to evaluate the extent of digital in the industry or even the ecosystem you operate in, it is equally important to understand the extent of digital in the society you operate."[7] A simple metric such as the number of networked (or connected) devices per person shows the disparity across geographical regions. For example, although there will be 3.6 networked devices per capita across the world by 2023, the number will vary from about 13.6 devices in the US to about 1.5 devices in India.[8] Such disparities in digitization—on both the supply side and the demand side—across different countries and regions imply the need for multinationals to carefully evaluate the intensity of digital forces for each of their major international markets.

Table 2.1 provides a simple checklist for managers to gauge the role digital technologies play in their company's business in a given international market. Do digital technologies play a critical role, a supportive or enabling role, or have limited influence on the business? The items in the checklist relate to the four key dimensions of global business that we identified in chapter 1—customers, ecosystem, operations, and resources. Managers should score the intensity of digital forces for each of the major international markets (industry-region combination) they operate in or plan to enter. A simple average of the scores for the twelve items will serve as a reasonably good indicator of the intensity of digital forces in that market.

Intensity of Regional and Local Forces

As we mentioned in chapter 1, forces of regionalization and geopolitical nationalism have swept across the world in the last several years.

Table 2.1

Intensity of digital forces

	In this market, the role of digital technologies in . . .	Limited		Enabling		Critical
Customer	1. . . . entering/connecting with new markets is:	1	2	3	4	5
	2. . . . engaging with customers is:	1	2	3	4	5
	3. . . . managing customer journeys is:	1	2	3	4	5
Ecosystem	4. . . . collaborating/cocreating value with partners is:	1	2	3	4	5
	5. . . . establishing a value creation platform is:	1	2	3	4	5
	6. . . . orchestrating the business ecosystem is:	1	2	3	4	5
Operations	7. . . . production and associated activities is:	1	2	3	4	5
	8. . . . supply chain and logistics activities is:	1	2	3	4	5
	9. . . . coordinating internal operations is:	1	2	3	4	5
Resources	10. . . . seeking/acquiring resources/ knowledge is:	1	2	3	4	5
	11. . . . pursuing innovation is:	1	2	3	4	5
	12. . . . corporate venturing activities is:	1	2	3	4	5

Such regional and local forces arise from an acute focus on localized concerns about job loss, national security, and income inequality and lead to policies at national and regional levels that favor or protect the interests of local companies. Regional and local forces may also arise from unique local conditions, including changing demographics, cultures, and political systems.

The intensity of such localized forces varies across different parts of the world. This is reflected in the findings from the DHL global connectedness index, which ranks countries on the extent to which they are connected (or integrated) with the rest of the world, as manifested by their participation in international flows of products and services (trade), capital, information, and people.[9] For instance, many of the Western European countries (such as the Netherlands, Switzerland, Belgium, Ireland, Denmark, the UK, and Germany) are ranked very high on global connectedness, whereas many African countries (Sudan, Zimbabwe, Uganda) fall at the bottom. Even within a continent, there is considerable variation. For example, while the UAE is ranked in the top ten in terms of global connectivity, other countries in the Middle East (such as Saudi Arabia, Oman, and Qatar) are less well connected and ranked below fifty.

Understanding the regional and local forces in an international market will require us to focus on the role and influence of local institutions, both formal and informal. From the perspective of formal institutions, we will consider trade regulations and policies (established by government agencies) and business and digital infrastructures (provided by public and private entities). From the perspective of informal institutions, we will consider the dominant business and consumer culture in that market. Let's now look at these in more detail.

Trade Regulations and Policies

Evidence of the regional and local forces at play in different parts of the world is available from the recent trade and technology policies announced by large emerging economies such as China and India. China has announced a set of policies and plans—including Made in China 2025, Thousand Talents Plan, and China's Fourteenth Five-Year Plan for Informatization (2021–2025)—that aim to protect and enhance the competitiveness of its local companies and to build a "digital Silk Road" that would allow for their dominance on regional trade. Similarly, India has adopted the Make in India initiative, covering twenty-five sectors of its economy and designed to foster innovation, protect intellectual property, and build best-in-class manufacturing infrastructure to enhance the competitiveness of local companies.

Italy, long a bastion of free trade, recently adopted measures (through an emergency decree) to expand the government's authority to veto meaningful foreign investment in any firm working in a wide range of industries, including electricity, water, health, media, data collection, aerospace, elections systems, banks, insurance, robotics, or biotechnology—in effect, closing the economy to foreign companies.[10]

Another indicator of the regional forces that are ascendant in different parts of the world is the ongoing negotiation among different countries on regional trade agreements (RTAs). For example, China, Japan, Australia, New Zealand, South Korea, and the ten ASEAN countries have been working on the Regional Comprehensive Economic Partnership (RCEP). Although India opted out of this pact, given that the pact's fifteen member nations account for nearly a third of the world's gross domestic product, RCEP will likely be a dominant regional trade agreement, with the potential to radically redefine the nature of global businesses and cross-border flows of goods and services. Similar regional efforts include the Comprehensive and Progressive Agreement for Trans-Pacific Partnership, formed after the US removed itself from the Trans-Pacific Partnership. As the WTO recently stated, the number and reach of regional trade agreements have steadily increased over the years. Currently, there are over three hundred regional trade agreements in force, indicating the overall intensity of regional and local forces operating across the world.[11]

Many countries are also in the process of regulating cross-border digital data flows, thereby introducing yet another significant type of localization force. For example, Russia's Federal Law 242-FZ requires companies to store Russian citizens' personal data on Russian servers and establishes an official registry to punish operators that fail to comply with the law. Similarly, China requires many types of data (generated by global companies from their operations in China) to be stored locally and also restricts digital imports in many areas. And India is currently in the process of instituting a data protection bill that would restrict cross-border movement of some types of business data.

In addition, many governments worldwide have adopted measures to restrict (or ban) foreign digital platforms in order to exercise greater control over digital speech and commerce. For example, the EU has started enforcing stricter regulation of US platform companies such as

Google and Apple; China has long banned Google, Facebook, and other US platforms; and, India recently banned several Chinese digital platforms, including TikTok and WeChat. While these and other regulations and measures are meant to protect consumer privacy (e.g., Australia's Personally Controlled Electronic Health Record restricts healthcare providers from exporting personally identifiable information), their broader impact has been on erecting new digital walls, reflecting the growing levels of techno-nationalism and protectionism present in different regions.[12]

Business and Digital Infrastructures

While digital technologies are inherently location-agnostic, recent initiatives in different parts of the world have focused on building regional (or localized) digital infrastructures that are limited to companies within a country or a region. For example, Softbank and Line, both of which are major digital platform players in Japan, recently announced a fifty-fifty merger to create a *super digital platform* that encompasses social media, chat, mobile commerce, and digital payments all in a single platform targeted exclusively at Japanese and Southeast Asian markets. In many other countries (including China and Russia), governments have taken the initiative to develop and/or promote regional digital infrastructures that are "partially closed" to global businesses in order to promote regional commerce, as well as enhance monitoring capabilities. As Bijoy Sagar, chief information technology and digital transformation officer at Bayer AG, told us, "A big part of this is the fear that one or two countries will end up holding much of the global digital real estate . . . and that it will not end well for everybody else."[13]

As digital technologies get infused into all types of common business infrastructures—from logistics and transportation systems to warehousing facilities to payment systems—it becomes easier for service providers in a country to constrain the access of such facilities to multinationals based on localized issues and political concerns. Further, even when such infrastructures and facilities are readily available, lack of adherence to global standards and/or lack of quality in many instances may preclude multinationals from utilizing them effectively.

Business and Consumer Culture

The growing nationalism evident across the world has also impacted consumer culture, driving a shift from global consumer culture to more local consumer culture in many markets.[14] For example, the *buy local* movement has gained popularity in major international markets such as the US, Germany, China, and India. Such consumer nationalism can also translate into supply-side practices that reflect preferences for local suppliers and partners.

Similarly, nationalistic and protectionist tendencies can also seep into the business culture in a country. It is well established that national culture can shape the corporate culture.[15] What has become evident in recent years is that in the long term, geopolitical tensions can also shape the corporate culture and the international relationships of companies in a country. A case in point is the ongoing trade conflict between the US and China. Arguably, over the past couple of years this has translated into more closed and less trusting stances adopted by companies on either side as they deal with one another. This impact on business culture can even percolate down into individual-level attitudes and behaviors (e.g., those of the local employees of a foreign multinational).

All of these factors indicate the different types of regional and local forces at play in the global business context. In table 2.2, we offer a simple checklist for managers to rate the intensity, along the three dimensions, of regional and local forces of a foreign market. The items relate to what extent the regulations/policies, infrastructure, and culture in a specific foreign market (industry/product and region combination) promote either globalization or localization. A simple average of the scores for the twelve items will serve as a reasonably good indicator of the intensity of regional and local forces in that foreign market.

A Typology of Global Business Contexts

Now that we know the intensity of digital forces and regional/local forces, we can consider them together to identify four unique contexts for global businesses (see figure 2.1). The average scores related to the intensity of digital forces and regional/local forces (calculated from

Table 2.2
Intensity of regional and local forces

	In this market . . .	Promote(s) globalization			Promote(s) localization	
Policies	1. Policies related to market entry by foreign companies:	1	2	3	4	5
	2. Trade treaties related to cross-border movement of goods:	1	2	3	4	5
	3. Policies related to IP and cross-border data flows:	1	2	3	4	5
	4. Policies related to competition with local companies:	1	2	3	4	5
Infrastructure	5. Production, logistics, and marketing infrastructures:	1	2	3	4	5
	6. Financial and capital investment infrastructures:	1	2	3	4	5
	7. Digital, communication, and data infrastructures:	1	2	3	4	5
	8. Access to local/regional business infrastructures:	1	2	3	4	5
Culture	9. The prevalent business culture of local companies:	1	2	3	4	5
	10. The prevalent consumer culture:	1	2	3	4	5
	11. The prevalent work culture of local employees:	1	2	3	4	5
	12. The prevalent innovation culture of local talent/partners:	1	2	3	4	5

tables 2.1 and 2.2) will help position a market in a specific quadrant. For example, if a particular international market scores 3.8 on digital forces and 1.7 on regional/local forces, it will belong to quadrant C.

Traditional localization (quadrant A) describes a market in which the regional and local forces are strong while the digital forces are still weak. Consider companies that strictly cater to regional markets. For example, there are hundreds of Chinese companies that manufacture low-end agricultural equipment and machinery for specific African countries (markets). These companies employ traditional manufacturing facilities

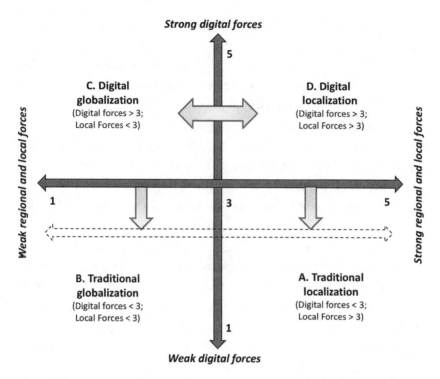

Figure 2.1

A typology of global business contexts

with limited digitization to produce their goods and exploit regional trade agreements that protect them from global competition to market those goods.

Traditional globalization (quadrant B) describes a market that exhibits weak digital forces and weak regional and local forces. Digital technologies are deployed by companies, but they are not critical and largely serve supportive roles (with minimal impact on business expansion decisions). Similarly, the market exists in a fairly globalized context (weak regional and local forces), so there is greater level of standardization or homogeneity in terms of market needs, as well as how value is created and delivered. Illustrative markets include low-value consumables and low-end apparel. In these markets, there have been limited digitization and homogenous customer needs, and the value chain is fairly globalized for companies to extract economies of scale. For example, Chinese companies that operate in the textile, apparel, and footwear markets have become key participants in the global value chain, assuming critical roles in production and distribution of cheap goods across the globe, but they operate with limited digitization.

The top left and right quadrants (C and D) in figure 2.1 denote markets in which the digital forces tend to be stronger. *Digital globalization* (quadrant C) involves markets in which there has been considerable digitization (on the supply side and/or the demand side) but regional and local forces have been relatively weak. In other words, these are markets in which digitization and globalization have converged, allowing companies to use different types of digital technologies and associated capabilities to expand their global presence in terms of operations or product/service delivery. For example, markets for many types of consumer electronics (including computing devices, mobile phones, and TVs) fall into this category. On the one hand, there have been relatively limited trade barriers and other protectionist measures for these markets, allowing companies such as Apple, OnePlus, and Samsung to cater to a globalized market with similar sets of products/services (and similar business models). But on the other hand, digital forces tend to be stronger, as varying types of digital technologies are used in manufacturing, logistics, and marketing, allowing companies to implement highly efficient and effective global supply chains and market-delivery systems. Recall the case of DJI, the Shenzhen-based global leader in the civilian drone industry that we mentioned in chapter 1. The company employs sophisticated digital capabilities—including robotics, digital platforms, mechatronics, and mobile technologies—as part of its offerings. At the same time, DJI has enjoyed the exploding global market (with increasing levels of market standardization and limited trade barriers) for civilian drones to fuel its rapid growth over the past ten years or so. These drones are now finding application in a wide range of areas, including the music and film industries.

Finally, *digital localization* (quadrant D) describes markets in which both digital forces and regional/local forces exercise considerable sway over global businesses. Consider the digital healthcare market. There is no question that digital technologies are revolutionizing the delivery of healthcare. From VR, AR, wearables, and IoT devices to analytics, AI, and mobile computing, digitization has allowed for radical changes in the ways in which personal health services are delivered, offering consumers anonymity, convenience, low-cost access, and round-the-clock support. The COVID-19 pandemic has only further expanded this digital health market. At the same time, the market for these and other personal healthcare solutions is highly localized, given that the business model for healthcare varies from one region/country to another and that government agencies play regulatory roles to different extents. For example, several countries have enacted laws (e.g., Australia's Personally Controlled Electronic Health Records Act of 2012) that govern where patient data is stored and how it is shared and processed. Such markets require companies to carefully evaluate each foreign market and position their offerings and business models based on local conditions.

Importantly, the global business landscape is very dynamic. As more powerful and versatile digital technologies get developed, their application areas keep expanding. As a result, industries and markets that were previously impervious to digitization may suddenly become susceptible to digital forces. The two downward-pointing arrows in figure 2.1 indicate the relentless advancement of digital technologies, conquering newer application domains and markets and thereby shrinking the traditional globalization and traditional localization quadrants. We assume here that it is quite unlikely that markets will become "undigitized"; that is, once digital technologies have been applied in a market, rarely will their influence wane.

On the other hand, the influence of regional and local forces may wax and wane. Previously localized markets may become more globalized and vice versa. The double-headed arrow in figure 2.1 indicates the constant transition of markets from quadrant C to quadrant D and vice versa. As we mentioned in chapter 1, Chinese smartphone manufacturer Xiaomi's rapid global growth has been supported by open global markets in Western Europe, Asia, and America. But more recently, some of these markets have become less open due to changing political and economic concerns, affecting the company's continued international growth. For example, the company had to temporarily leave the Brazilian market due to increased economic instability. Similarly, its plans to enter the US market in 2019 had to be put on hold amid the rising US-China trade tensions. In mid-2020, growing India-China political tensions led to the ban of Xiaomi's apps in India.

As we noted at the beginning of this chapter in the global auto industry example, the variation in digital and regional/local forces may place different international markets in an industry in different quadrants. For instance, while the overall digital maturity of the US and the EU auto markets is high—that is, the major auto companies and their ecosystem partners have digitized their operations to a considerable extent—in the Indian auto industry, digitization is less consistent across the value chain. There, the large auto companies have digitized their operations, but many Indian OEMs are behind the curve in digital investments.[16] The implication of all this is that a company operating in the auto industry and pursuing global expansion may find that some of its target markets for international expansion are highly globalized and digitized (and thus fall in quadrant C) while some others are localized (falling in quadrants A or D). This calls for different approaches in terms of market entry, customer acquisition, partner management, knowledge acquisition, and operations.

How should companies navigate such a dynamic and varied global business landscape? We suggest that companies can implement different types of digital global business connectivity, as discussed next, to fit the nature of the foreign markets they desire to expand to.

Digital Global Business Connectivity

Now we'll explain in more detail the concept of digital global business connectivity that we introduced in chapter 1. Let's start with its conceptual foundation—the notion of tight and loose coupling.

Tight and Loose Coupling: The Conceptual Foundation for Digital Global Business Connectivity

Tight and *loose coupling* describe the extent of dependencies between two entities. If two entities are loosely coupled, they have low levels of dependency on each other; when they are tightly coupled, they are highly dependent on each other. This simple idea has found application in a wide range of fields, from software design to organizational design to business model design. For example, in computing and systems design, a loosely coupled architecture is desirable to keep maintenance costs low, as making a change in one part of the system is less likely to disrupt other parts of the system (i.e., lower dependencies imply less of a ripple effect across the system). Thus, loose coupling enhances the overall flexibility of the system to respond to external changes as it is easier and more cost-effective to make those changes. It also allows the system to cater to different use contexts (different sets of user needs) because different variations of a component can be plugged into the same system and behave differently in different contexts. Yet in some instances, a tight coupling might be desirable as it allows for more efficient and stable operations. Tightly coupled systems architecture can reduce the extent of information that needs to be shared between different elements/components (because they have better awareness of each other), thereby increasing the speed with which the system operates. Tighter coupling also makes the system more closed, thereby enhancing its overall integrity and stability. Thus, tight and loose coupling reflect the trade-offs between efficiency and stability on one side and flexibility and adaptability on the other side.

Drawing on this general idea, we consider tight and loose coupling as highlighting the balance between responsiveness and distinctiveness in a multinational's global business context (see figure 2.2).[17] As we briefly noted in chapter 1, *responsiveness* relates to the need for the different foreign subsidiaries, partners, or parts of a multinational to be responsive to or be aligned with one another, whereas *distinctiveness* relates to the need for the individual subsidiaries and partners to adapt to and reflect the distinctive or unique aspects of the local market context.

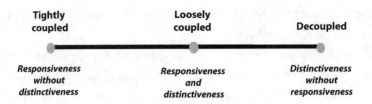

Figure 2.2
Tight and loose coupling

First, let's look at the option at the far right end. If there is distinctiveness but no responsiveness—which implies that the system behaves differently but lacks coherence among the different units—then the system is decoupled. In a decoupled system, there are no connections or relationships at all between the different parts, with each part behaving independently. Multinationals can rarely operate in such a fashion, and as such we will not consider decoupling as a strategic option in this book.

If a system is at the far left—that is, it has responsiveness but no distinctiveness, which implies that it can respond efficiently but not differently—the system is said to be tightly coupled. If there are both distinctiveness *and* responsiveness, in the middle, then the system is loosely coupled. In a loosely coupled system, the different parts of the system are connected to one another (coupled) and thereby contribute to a certain extent of responsiveness. At the same time, there is looseness in those connections or relationships, which in turn contributes to a certain extent of distinctiveness. But note that although loose coupling does involve responsiveness, it may not be to the extent that is possible or evident in a tightly coupled system. Thus, in this book we will consider cases in which tight coupling provides the best avenue for achieving digital global business connectivity, as well as those in which loose coupling is the preferred avenue.

Importantly, the extent of desired responsiveness and distinctiveness is dependent on the intensity and location of the uncertainty that resides outside the system. Higher levels of uncertainty may call for looser coupling, whereas lower levels of uncertainty permit tighter coupling. However, a system may face higher levels of uncertainty in certain respects and lower levels of uncertainty in other respects. For example, consider the business model in the fast-food industry. Chains such as McDonald's and Pizza Hut have focused on tight coupling in their supply chains, store design, and delivery of user experiences so as to enjoy gains related to efficiency and scale of operations. At the same time, as they expand to newer international markets, the need for more diverse offerings calls for employing looser coupling related to menu creation and maintenance, sourcing, and supplier selection. Thus, tight coupling and loose coupling can coexist within the same company.

We build our concept of digital global business connectivity on the tight and loose coupling idea. In so doing, we elaborate on how managers can evaluate the need for such tight coupling or loose coupling in different international business markets and devise an appropriate set of digital global business strategies.

Digital Global Business Connectivity and Global Business Strategies

As we briefly stated in chapter 1, digital global business connectivity incorporates the nature of a company's relationships—built on digital technologies and associated capabilities—into global customers and markets, global partners and ecosystems, global activities and operations, and global resources and knowledge. Across these four dimensions, we can identify seven different elements of digital global business connectivity.

Table 2.3 lists these seven elements of digital global business connectivity; we will examine each of these seven elements in detail in chapters 3–6.

Broadly, these seven elements of digital global business connectivity reflect the choices that a company makes with regard to seeking, establishing, and managing (or governing) those relationships. The specific choices that a company makes with regard to all of these will become visible through its global business strategies—strategies related to foreign market entry, customer engagement, platform and ecosystem governance, production and supply chain operations, innovation and

Table 2.3
Elements of digital global business connectivity

Dimension	Element of digital global business connectivity	Description
Global customers and markets	*Company-market connectivity*	Relates to a company's mode of entry into a foreign market, including sales channels and operations
	Brand-customer connectivity	Relates to how a company manages its brand in a foreign market and how its customers engage with the brand
Global partners and ecosystems	*Platform-market connectivity*	Relates to how a company's digitized business platform connects with a foreign market in terms of its value proposition, digital assets, and data infrastructure
	Company-ecosystem connectivity	Relates to how a company manages relationships with its partners in a foreign market and orchestrates value creation in the ecosystem
Global activities and operations	*Company-subsidiary connectivity*	Relates to a company's relationship with its subsidiaries in different countries and reflects the coordination processes and the allocation of decision-making powers
Global resources and knowledge	*Company-innovation source connectivity*	Relates to a company's overall approach to seeking and sourcing innovation from a foreign market
	Company-innovation asset connectivity	Relates to how a company reconfigures and deploys the innovation assets generated in a foreign market, along with its other assets and resources

knowledge acquisition, business model innovation, and corporate venturing, which are, in turn, realized in practice through the application of diverse sets of digital technology capabilities.

Importantly, a company's digital global business connectivity will depend on the nature of the international business context—specifically, on the intensity of regional/local forces in terms of government regulations/policies, digital and business infrastructure, and business and consumer culture. For example, how a company identifies, connects with, and manages its relationships with customers in a foreign market may depend on how globalized or localized the market entry policies and/or the consumer culture are in that market. The greater the extent of globalization, the tighter the coupling that is possible between the company and its foreign market operations. On the other hand, more localized contexts would likely demand loose coupling, with greater levels of distinctiveness in how the company adapts to local conditions. As such, the specific strategic choices related to each of the elements of digital global business connectivity (shown in table 2.3) will need to be contingent on the intensity of regional/local forces.

In short, digital global business connectivity provides a broad framework for a company to devise and deploy a comprehensive and coherent set of global business strategies that are founded on digital technology capabilities and suited to different international market contexts.

Now, let's try to put all of this together. Managers pursuing international expansion of their businesses will need to ask themselves three questions. First: *What is the nature of the target foreign market?* Or where is it situated on the digital forces and regional or local forces landscape (figure 2.1)? An evaluation of this can be made using the scales provided in tables 2.1 and 2.2. By plotting the average scores for the intensity of digital forces and regional/local forces, you can locate the market in the digital forces and regional or local forces landscape. This can help reveal whether the target foreign market involves digital globalization or digital localization and hence the extent of tight coupling or loose coupling between the company and its foreign market operations.

Second: *What specific global business strategies should the company adopt to achieve the desired digital global business connectivity?* A company's move into a particular international market may emphasize one or more of the four dimensions and related elements of digital global business connectivity. Thus, for each of the relevant elements of digital global business connectivity, the company will need to select strategies based on whether the foreign market demands globalization or localization. In the chapters ahead, we will focus on each of the dimensions and related elements of digital global business connectivity, and we'll discuss alternative business strategies and their fit based on the intensity of localization forces.

And third: *What are the capabilities that correspond to these business strategies?* Implementation of the different digital global business strategies will call for not only acquiring the requisite digital technology capabilities but also, importantly, integrating such capabilities with other organizational capabilities. In the chapters ahead, we'll use examples and case studies to illustrate the different capabilities that underlie digital global business connectivity.

Companies also have to ensure that the broader portfolios of such digital global business strategies that they come up with are sufficiently coherent and consistent with one another (i.e., there is not too much disparity in terms of the business risks they entail, and the company's organizational identity is consistent across different international markets). Such portfolio-level considerations assume greater significance as companies pursue rapid-growth strategies in which decisions made for one foreign market may set up path dependencies and influence the company's performance in other foreign markets.

Consider the case of India's leading multinational conglomerate, the Aditya Birla Group (ABG). Based in Mumbai, with revenues of US$48 billion, ABG operates in thirty-four countries and a wide range of markets, including cement, metals, viscose staple fiber, branded apparel, chemicals, fertilizers, and telecom. Given that ABG pursues businesses in both globalized and localized markets and in very diverse sectors, there is a high probability that its global business strategies—in different regions and sectors—are inconsistent with one another and limit the company's overall ability to pursue international growth opportunities in the future. To address this, ABG recently embarked on a strategy built on digital technology capabilities (including AI and data analytics) to modularize and digitize core processes and operational assets across its different businesses, using predictive maintenance, sales forecasting, customer churn and promotion tracking, and freight optimization to make these processes and assets more portable across borders. These digitally enabled core assets can then be rapidly customized to fit different international businesses contexts and reused to enhance the overall consistency of the company's approach to operations. We will discuss these and other strategies in more detail in later chapters. But as Deep Thomas, group chief data and analytics officer at ABG, noted, the goal is to build business-agnostic digital capabilities and assets that could be rapidly reconfigured and extended to any foreign market context without losing the overall coherence at the corporate level.[18]

Such an approach also reflects the core message of our book: multinationals need to adapt their growth and expansion strategies to fit different foreign market conditions by employing the affordances that digital technologies provide to connect with customers, partners, operations, and resources in flexible ways. In short, initiatives such as ABG's indicate the potential and promise of anchoring a company's global expansion strategy to its digital global business connectivity.

Now that we have a better understanding of the global business landscape framed by digital and regional/local forces, we will proceed with our analysis focused on the four key dimensions of digital global business connectivity: customers and markets, partners and ecosystems, activities and operations, and resources and knowledge. For each dimension, we will describe the key elements, associated digital global business strategies, and underlying capabilities.

We start with a focus on global customers and markets.

3 Connecting with Global Markets and Customers Digitally

Burberry, a British luxury fashion house with annual revenues of $2.75 billion, has always prided itself on the exclusivity of its offerings (reflected in its "timeless authenticity" theme) and has catered to its global customers through physical stores that allow the company to preserve the aura of luxury. The company has around five hundred stores the world over, and even when the company adopted its "go digital" initiative and established the Burberry World website in the late 2000s, physical stores continued to be the anchor to engage with customers. But when Burberry became serious about the Chinese market, it decided to pursue a different strategy—one that relied heavily on *local digital channels*. Once the company bought out the operations from its franchisee, Kwok Hang Holdings of Hong Kong (paying about $87 million), it struck up a partnership with the Chinese e-commerce giant Alibaba and opened a virtual store on Alibaba's Tmall site. Tmall is known for heavy discounts and knockoffs, not for high-end offerings. While the move risked cheapening the brand, Burberry was focused on drawing in younger Chinese shoppers who shop mostly online. The company also chose WeChat as the primary venue for advertising, sales, and customer service. For example, the company conducted twenty-four-hour flash sales on WeChat.

Burberry's strategies, which relied on regional/local digital channels to enter the Chinese market, may seem pioneering among luxury houses, but they are in no way limited to that sector or to that country. Indeed, in recent years a wide range of multinational companies—including

BMW, Lululemon, Unilever, Nike, Harman International, and Procter & Gamble—have adopted similar strategies to enter and engage with customers in China, India, and other Asian markets.

This approach illustrates two key issues that are central to this chapter. First, the growing intensity of regional and local forces is forcing companies to rethink their global marketing strategies and to adopt more localized approaches. Second, much of the rethinking is predicated on the rapidly changing digital landscape that allows companies to radically change the ways by which they enter and connect with customers in different foreign markets. The exponential growth in the use of digital channels by customers the world over as a result of the COVID-19 pandemic has further accelerated this trend. The case of luxury brands—which typically prefer physical stores to emphasize exclusivity—serves to exemplify the acuteness of such digital and localization forces that are transforming the international sales and marketing strategies of companies of every stripe.

In this chapter, we explore two related questions: How are globalization and localization forces shaping multinational companies' market entry and customer connection strategies? And how are these strategies being redefined by digital technologies and platforms?

Multinational enterprises have always faced (and struggled with) the question of whether their international marketing and brand strategies should be global or local. Should they extend the marketing mix to all markets or adjust it to suit local markets? This question has sparked significant debate (the standardization versus localization debate), and ultimately many companies have reached a compromise called *glocal marketing* ("think global, act local"), as first suggested by Honda Motors.[1] For example, Apple Stores around the world follow a customer service protocol that is customized for and aligned with the culture of each region. The Paris Apple Store is housed in a Haussmann-type building that is suited to Parisians' tastes in architecture. Bob Bridger, former vice president of Apple's retail development, noted that "once a location is picked, it's all a matter of working towards making sure the store has an inviting appeal that matches its surrounding culture and environment. It's about 'getting out into the street' and feeling what the local feels."[2] So what's different now?

First, as we discussed in chapter 2, the intensity of regional and local forces have increased considerably over the past few years, making it imperative to rethink the nature and extent of such localized approaches. The type of localized marketing strategies that companies adopted in prior years—for example, changing the physical store setup as in Apple's case or the product mix as in McDonald's case—are no longer adequate or even appropriate. More fundamental changes in business models, structures, and processes are needed.

This is becoming evident along three key dimensions: government policies and regulations, digital and marketing infrastructures, and consumer culture. Government policies and regulations have created a number of barriers for foreign market entry, requiring companies to adopt newer approaches. For example, the foreign direct investment (FDI) policies in India have become more liberal over the years, yet they still require 30 percent of the value of goods to be procured from India if the foreign entity has an FDI exceeding 51 percent.[3]

Similarly, in many foreign markets the uniqueness or peculiarities of the regional and local infrastructure for marketing and sales operations—for example, the relative lack of popularity of credit cards and the increasing use of regional digital wallets as payment mechanisms in the Indian market—have made it difficult for companies to maintain their reliance on common global infrastructures and business models. In some foreign markets, even the digital infrastructure is localized, as illustrated by the dominance of domestic social media platforms in China.

Further, the ascendance of economic nationalism has only deepened the rift between the global consumer culture and the local consumer culture and heightened the importance of local consumer values.[4] For example, in India, the Make in India (Swadeshi) and the Vocal for Local movements have increased consumers' interest and excitement in products with local roots. Such local cultural affinity is vividly illustrated by the popularity of micromultinationals such as Forest Essentials (an Indian cosmetics company that specializes in Ayurveda-based products) and Fabindia (a retail chain that offers products handmade by craftspeople across rural India). Indeed, a recent report noted that 60 percent of Indian consumers were willing to pay extra for products that are locally made.[5] As Harish Bijoor, a leading brand-strategy consultant in India, told us, "The shift in the consumer culture towards more locally sourced products that started in rural India in around 2016 and spread to the urban parts has benefited local producers considerably."[6]

Many novel strategies and approaches to international marketing are enabled by advances in digital technologies. Digital technologies enhance the degrees of freedom that companies have in managing the coupling between their global and local marketing strategies. For example, the world of social media and brand influencers allow companies to tightly or loosely couple their marketing in distant parts of the world to their global brand, based on a host of conditions, including market heterogeneity, sociopolitical governance, and extent of unbranded competition. In parallel with this, digital technologies and data analytics have rapidly enhanced firms' capabilities to derive valuable insights into customer engagement based on near-real-time data. For example, intelligent connectivity technologies (5G, IoT, AI) have shortened the distance between physical and digital channels, allowing multinationals to engage with their foreign customers in ways that are meaningful in the local market context. In short, digital technologies and analytics are driving global customer engagement on a scale and with complexity never witnessed before.

To better understand how companies can fashion their international market entry and customer strategies to fit particular foreign markets using digital technologies, we need to first consider the key elements of digital global business connectivity.

Elements of Tight and Loose Coupling with Global Markets and Customers

We define two elements of a company's *digital global business connectivity* with regard to international markets and customers: company-market connectivity and brand-customer connectivity.

The first element, *company-market connectivity*, relates to a company's overall approach to international market selection and mode of entry, including sales channels and operations. Traditionally, firms have employed several modes of entry, ranging from nonequity, arm-length connections (franchise, licensing) to equity-based direct connections (foreign subsidiaries). Digital technologies have expanded these options for market entry, including their timing, scale, and scope. The emergence of various forms of digital sales channels has given rise to new possibilities for customer engagement. Such digital channels can coexist with more traditional physical channels, and the extent of integration between digital and physical channels determines the possibilities for tight and loose coupling. Importantly, the different approaches can be calibrated based on the ambiguity of the external environment (e.g., regulatory and economic conditions) allowing for varying degrees of tight and loose coupling.

The second element, *brand-customer connectivity*, relates to how a firm manages its brand and how international customers relate to it. Brands can be global or regional/local, and digital technologies offer new possibilities for firms to manage the global and local variations of their brands, as well as for customers to engage with the brands. Cultural and other regional/local factors shape how a firm may practice tight or loose coupling with regard to brand-customer connectivity.

In each of these elements, tight coupling represents greater levels of standardization and control (e.g., in sales operations, branding, decision processes) across the enterprise and hence greater responsiveness to changes in corporate-level priorities and strategies in other markets. At the same time, such tight coupling could lead to considerable disconnect between a company's customer strategies in a foreign market and the local conditions. Loose coupling, on the other hand, allows for applying local perspectives and solutions in order to adapt to local conditions, thereby contributing to more distinctiveness.

Next, we consider these two elements in more detail.

Company-Market Connectivity and International Market Entry Strategies

Digital Channels as a Mode of Foreign Market Entry

Typically, companies opt to enter a foreign market with an arm's-length approach (e.g., franchise operations) and then decide to bring the operation inside—to buy out the franchise and establish a wholly owned subsidiary—so as to establish tighter control over the brand. However, digital channels have opened up alternatives to the traditional arm's-length approaches by offering new direct avenues to conduct sales and marketing operations. Global business-to-consumer (B2C) e-commerce sales were $3.5 trillion in 2019 (14.1 percent of total retail sales) and are expected to exceed $6.5 trillion by 2023.[7] Even in a market such as India that has lagged global ecommerce trends, online retail sales are expected to double from $32 billion in 2019 to about $66 billion by 2024.[8] As noted previously, the COVID-19 crisis has accelerated these growth trends considerably.

Digital channels may seemingly favor strong global brands, but even firms with less prominent brand recognition have effectively used digital channels in prior years. For example, both Dollar Shave Club and Harry's (the customers of which subscribe to monthly deliveries of razor blades and other personal grooming products) exploited digital channels to expand to foreign markets dominated by Gillette, such as Canada, the United Kingdom, and Australia.[9] Similarly, Chinese luxury Mongolian cashmere brand Sand River has several brick-and-mortar stores in China, but when it decided to expand to international markets, it relied exclusively on digital channels. And by 2019, its overseas sales—all through the digital sales channel—accounted for close to 15 percent of its revenues.

Such digital channels can offer varying levels of control and access to customers. On the one hand, companies such as Apple and Samsung have established dedicated brand websites to allow customers in foreign markets to purchase their products online. Such websites allow companies to exercise considerable control over their product marketing mix and brand, but they have the drawback that a company needs to figure out the logistics of getting its products to customers in foreign markets. At the other extreme, e-retailers such as Amazon act as resellers; they purchase products from other companies and resell them to customers in different foreign markets. This allows companies—especially small businesses—to get their products into foreign markets with minimal investment and risk. But in addition to getting lower margins, companies also have no direct access to their foreign customers, putting into question the viability of their long-term international expansion agenda.

In between these two extremes, there is a sweet spot that holds considerable promise for large and small companies as they ponder expansion to foreign markets via digital channels, especially markets that are subject to considerable regional and local forces. This option is to have dedicated brand stores on digital marketplaces, which could be global (Amazon) or regional (Tmall, Flipkart, Pinduoduo, Mercado Libre). Such dedicated brand stores permit considerable control over brand and marketing mixes and allow for direct access to customers. While the global digital channels enable a greater degree of standardization across countries, regional/local digital channels permit access to niche foreign markets. At the same time, a significant part of order fulfilment and other local distribution operations can be parceled out to the online marketplace. For example, Amazon Global Selling offers a wide range of sales and marketing services, including order management and fulfilment, customer support, and, more importantly, international registration, taxes, and payments. Some of these services are not cheap, but they do enable companies (especially smaller companies) to enter and test the water in international markets that they are not sure about.

Tight and Loose Coupling between Physical and Digital Channels

Our research shows two broad strategies for multinationals to connect with foreign markets based on the extent of localization: global channel integration and digital first (see table 3.1). While the first strategy relates to globalized markets, the second suits more localized markets.

Table 3.1
Strategies for company-market connectivity

Strategy	Intensity of localization forces			Nature of coupling
	Government regulations and policies	Marketing and digital infrastructure	Consumer culture	
Global channel integration	Low	Low	Low to moderate	Tight coupling
Digital first	Moderate to high	Moderate to high	High	Loose coupling

Global channel integration involves entering and operating in a foreign market by investing in both physical and digital channels and adopting the multinational's global (or standardized) operational model to enhance efficiency and responsiveness.

Consider a fairly globalized foreign market, one that is highly embedded in the global trade and poses limited local/regional trade barriers. The marketing infrastructure (e.g., payment systems, product distribution systems) tends to be standardized, posing limited barriers for a company to port its sales and marketing structures and processes from elsewhere in the globalized world. The absence of localized trade policies and regulations and the relatively well-defined and predictable institutional influences imply greater business stability and a lower risk for multinationals to pursue foreign direct investment. Consumer values and norms in such markets also tend to be well aligned with global consumer culture. Overall, the global nature of the market implies reduced need for distinctiveness in terms of sales processes and operations and the potential for multinationals to plan for long-term investments in physical stores and, importantly, to integrate them with their global digital channels.

Lululemon, a $4 billion Canadian athletic apparel multinational that operates in North America, Europe, and some parts of the Asia Pacific region, has pursued such a global channel integration strategy. Launched in 1998, the company fueled much of its early international growth by sticking to globalized markets—primarily the US, Australia, the UK, and New Zealand. This allowed the company to invest in corporate-owned stores (by 2014, there were around 289 stores in these four countries) and to bring a unique approach to all its physical stores—one that positions the stores as "trend hubs" aimed to showcase the wellness lifestyle behind the athletic wear brand, as well as platforms to connect with local communities and serve as conversation starters.

Although the physical stores formed the primary customer touchpoints, Lululemon also established a global digital sales channel as early as 2009. The growth in direct-to-customer digital channels has been steady, contributing more than a quarter of the company's total revenue by 2019. And starting around 2015, the company also launched initiatives focused on bringing together its physical and digital channels more explicitly. Specifically, the company started integrating customer data from every digital and physical channel in order to provide insights into all aspects of customer behavior—from purchases to customer reviews on social media—allowing it to offer a coherent and personalized customer experience.

Researchers have studied how such integration across digital and physical channels would enable a company to speak with one voice across a customer's journey, thereby offering more coherent customer experiences, and in turn, enhancing customer engagement and loyalty.[10] Increasingly, customer journeys involve both types of channels and in interspersed ways. Companies that can analyze and learn from customer interaction data from both venues in real time and use such insights to manage future interactions have much to gain. New digital and analytic technologies, including VR/AR, 5G, IoT, and AI, allow companies to do just that. For example, multinationals can use data acquired from customer interactions in digital and physical channels to offer highly contextualized in-store experiences (e.g., smart fitting rooms, virtual reality merchandising). In 2019, Lululemon launched a new digital initiative to offer such integrated guest experiences across channels "intended to inspire, provoke and celebrate guests who live a healthy and mindful lifestyle."[11] Similarly, when Birchbox, the online beauty products retailer, branched out to physical presence, the company focused on integrating customers' physical and digital shopping experiences and making them more "holistic, seamless and designed to help shoppers make informed, confident decisions."[12] Sephora and other beauty retailers have also moved toward integrating their physical and digital channels to offer more seamless customer experiences. It is evident that bringing together a company's high-tech and high-touch customer interactions (e.g., to facilitate *webrooming*, in which customers first research products online before buying them in a physical store, and *showrooming*, in which customers try out products in a physical store before ultimately purchasing online) has clear advantages.[13]

However, such a strategy that involves establishing physical stores in a foreign market and integrating them with the company's global digital channels is largely predicated on operating in globalized market environments that offer higher levels of predictability, particularly with regard to trade policies and digital infrastructure and regulations. When local and regional forces hold considerable sway and imbue a great amount of market uncertainty—in terms of institutional roles and their influence, digital infrastructure, and/or consumer values and norms—the *digital-first* strategy is more appropriate.

For example, when Lululemon expanded to China, it didn't initially follow the strategy that it had followed to that point in the United States, Australia, and other such markets. Instead, it started with a digital presence on Chinese e-commerce platform Tmall in 2015. It built three showrooms in Beijing and Shanghai in 2013, but those were largely for marketing purposes—to hype the brand and to build awareness by hosting yoga, cardio, and kickboxing events. The company relied largely on its regional digital channels (Tmall, WeChat) to drive sales in China, and it was quite successful. Many other multinationals—including Michigan-based vacuum cleaner manufacturer Bissell and New Zealand-America footwear start-up Allbirds—have followed suit by focusing on digital platforms first when entering the Chinese market.

Such a digital-first strategy allows companies to gain a presence in a foreign market when the prevailing conditions—in particular, trade policies and regulations—are not very conducive for establishing a physical presence. Consider Apple's evolving strategy in India. Until very recently, Apple sold its products in India largely through regional e-commerce platforms such as Flipkart and Paytm Mall. However, recent changes made in the country's FDI rules allowed the company to establish its own online store and reach out to customers directly. But even now, until it sets up its own physical stores across the country (the first few physical stores will be limited to large cities such as Mumbai), the company will continue to market its products through third-party physical stores, with limited integration between the digital and physical channels. Indeed, the peculiarities of the Indian market, combined with continued ambiguity about government FDI policies, emphasize the significance of digital channels rather than corporate-owned physical stores to reach potential customers.

Further, the emergence of powerful regional e-commerce platforms has made digital-first strategies very appealing to foreign multinationals as risk-averse avenues for international expansion. Consider Jio Platforms, a holding company for all the digital businesses of the Indian conglomerate, Reliance Industries Limited. It includes the Jio mobile data network, India's largest mobile network (with over four hundred million subscribers), offering the world's cheapest fare for mobile data connectivity.[14] The market-facing platforms—including JioMart, an online grocery delivery platform—built on top of this network infrastructure provide a wide range of digital services. Recently, both Facebook and Google have joined these efforts by acquiring minority stakes in Jio Platforms with the goal of providing customized versions of their offerings for Jio customers. For example, Google's customized version of its Android operating system will drive a low-cost, entry-level smartphone (manufactured by Reliance), and Facebook's WhatsApp (which has around two hundred million users in India) will offer a host of services, including order payment. Reliance is now getting thousands of local *kiranas* (small, neighborhood retail stores) to set up their online presence on JioMart so that consumers can place (and pay for) orders on WhatsApp and get their products delivered by the local stores—in effect, creating a seamless e-commerce platform that merges the power and convenience of digital platforms with the reach and "localness" of the kiranas. Such a comprehensive regional platform would form an ideal vehicle for foreign multinationals to rapidly establish a digital presence in India and reach Indian consumers (both urban and rural) in a cost-effective way.

The gradual tightening of foreign investment and trade policies, as well as the increasing dominance of integrated, regional, digital e-commerce platforms in different parts of the world, has paved the way for multinationals to adopt digital-first strategies when entering new international markets. But it should be noted that a digital-first strategy doesn't imply that companies have to stick to digital venues for the long term. As their growth in foreign markets increases and as they gain more confidence in managing regional/local forces, multinationals could extend their presence to physical stores too. For example, after their initial foray into the Chinese market through digital channels, both Burberry and Lululemon opened physical stores in a few locations in China.

Even when such physical channels are launched in a localized foreign market, in general, the benefits from integrating digital and physical channels may not outweigh the risks associated with the localization forces (e.g., stability of FDI policies). For example, Swedish clothing retailer H&M and a host of other European consumer brands were recently caught in the crossfire between EU and China regarding the alleged human-rights violations in the Xinjiang region. The backlash from the Chinese government was particularly severe for H&M as overnight it was effectively erased from all regional e-commerce platforms, rendering the company without a direct digital link to the vast Chinese market. Over five hundred of the company's physical stores across China were also boycotted and even disappeared from the map services operated by Alibaba and Baidu.[15] But in certain instances, companies may decide to pursue limited levels of integration between their physical and digital venues. For example, on digital venues such as Tmall, rogue actors often offer counterfeits and companies may risk brand dilution. To partly respond to such localized risks, in China, Burberry has started partnering with Tencent. They are blending social media and retail to create physical spaces (with the first one in Shenzhen, China's technology hub) in which engaged customers can interact, share, and shop. The broader strategy for Burberry is to leverage the customer access offered by regional digital platforms (such as WeChat) and to integrate that with physical channels so as to offer distinctive (localized) customer experiences that will also, importantly, serve to protect the brand.

Thus, though global channel integration broadly implies tight coupling that involves higher levels of standardization and responsiveness across a multinational's operations in different foreign markets, a digital-first strategy emphasizes loose coupling that indicates distinctiveness in a foreign market (e.g., by embedding sales operations in regional digital infrastructure) without sacrificing responsiveness. However, as should be evident from our discussion so far, these two alternatives are meant to be prototypical strategies that incorporate several different factors. For example, should a company enter a market via physical and/or digital channels? If digital, should they be global digital platforms or regional digital platforms? If the company pursues both digital and physical venues, should they be integrated? If so, to what extent and for what purposes? With different combinations of these factors, companies can create different flavors of the two strategies—digital-first and global channel integration—to suit the nature of localization forces in a market and achieve different levels of tight/loose coupling for digital global business connectivity.

Brand-Customer Connectivity and the Orchestration of International Marketing

Digital Platforms and Brand Building in International Markets
Brand-customer connectivity, the second element of digital global business connectivity, relates to how a company manages its brand in foreign markets and how its international customers relate to it.

Brands serve several key roles in international markets, both in B2C and B2B markets. Apart from enabling customers to realize their aspirational goals, brands make it easier for customers to make purchase decisions because a brand's reputation can enhance customer trust and reduce risk. As such, this limits the time and effort needed on the part of consumers to make a careful evaluation of a product. This is particularly important in foreign markets, where companies may enjoy limited access to (or interactions with) their customers and the brand becomes the primary vehicle to conduct those interactions. The advent of digital platforms and technologies have transformed how multinationals conduct such brand-related interactions with foreign customers (or how foreign customers engage with brands).[16]

Traditionally, companies used to make considerable investment in local television and print media to introduce and build their brands in each foreign market. This took considerable time and effort, making it a slow and gradual process. Digital platforms (e.g., social media) have enhanced both the speed and the scope of international brand building. A wide range of digital platforms with global or regional reach—including social media (e.g., Facebook, Twitter, Instagram, WeChat, Weibo), online review platforms (e.g., Yelp, Baidu Tieba, Manta, MouthShut), and e-commerce platforms (e.g., Amazon, eBay, Tmall)—allow consumers to communicate with companies and with peers about their brand experiences via reviews, likes, and posts. Further, most consumers are passive participants in brand-related interactions; by and large, they consume rather than produce brand-related information. Often, a small minority of consumers assume an outsized role in shaping those conversations and, in turn, enjoy considerable influence over how the brand is perceived by other consumers (and influence on others' purchase behavior). Generally referred to as *influencers* (or digital opinion leaders), these consumers can be either global or local in their reach and influence and can serve as a potent vehicle to introduce and/ or redefine brands in foreign markets.

All of these brand-related interactions made possible by digital platforms have led to two issues that are of particular interest to us in considering foreign markets. First, they have brought to the fore the need to understand the differences (if any) between the global consumer culture and the local consumer culture (specific to a foreign market). While digital platforms allow brand-related conversations to go global, it would be wrong to assume that they reduce the significance of local consumer culture (or lead to the dominance of global consumer culture). Indeed, as mentioned previously, one of the outcomes of the ascendance of nationalistic forces has been a consumer culture that is more tightly embedded in the local values and norms of a country or region. This in turn implies the need to consider the perceived localness of a brand or how the brand is perceived by consumers in a foreign market.

Second, the speed with which brand perceptions flow across national borders on digital platforms also raises the issue of how brand-related events that occur in a foreign market affect the global brand (and vice versa). Historically, most companies have assumed that such contagion effects are minimal (a company's actions in one country have little effect on how it is perceived in another country). Digital platforms have made that no longer true: both positive and negative contagion effects are quite evident.

More broadly, the nature of the connection between the global brand and the local brand becomes a key design element in shaping the brand-customer connectivity in different foreign markets.

Tight and Loose Coupling in Brand-Customer Connectivity

We interpret brand-customer connectivity in terms of the integration between a company's global brand and local brand in response to the intensity of regional/local forces in a specific foreign market. Two broad types of strategies are possible: *digital globalness*, which involves tight coupling, and *digital culturation*, which implies loose coupling (see table 3.2).

A digital globalness strategy involves establishing a tight connection between a global brand and the customers in a foreign market. Consider a globalized foreign market in which the global consumer culture

Table 3.2
Strategies for brand-customer connectivity

Strategy	Intensity of localization forces			Nature of coupling
	Government regulations and policies	Digital infrastructure	Consumer culture	
Digital globalness	Low to moderate	Low	Low	Tight coupling
Digital culturation	High	Moderate to high	Moderate to high	Loose coupling

is dominant, thereby rendering local consumer culture less influential. As such, companies can emphasize their brand's globalness—that is, their global imagery—and value systems, which in turn implies fairly standardized marketing and brand communication initiatives. Local adaptations of the brand are not needed and may even detract from the core brand message that the company intends to convey.

This can be achieved in different ways. For instance, multinationals can employ global influencers and opinion leaders to develop a global following for their brands and then use that to enhance their product's market appeal in a foreign market. A wide range of global influencers—including celebrities (Mariah Carey, Kylie Jenner), sports stars (Cristiano Ronaldo), actors (George Clooney), and musicians (Taylor Swift)—have been employed by companies to this end. Multinational companies such as Airbnb, Lululemon, and Pinkberry have all used global influencers in establishing their global brand. For example, when Mariah Carey stayed in an Airbnb mansion in 2015, the company famously used the opportunity to employ her as a celebrity influencer (Carey's post on Instagram got more than forty-five thousand likes). Following that initial effort, Airbnb has used celebrity influencers to establish the globalness of its brand via Instagram's seven hundred million active users.

Even in B2B markets, the influence of such global opinion leaders has become critical. Companies such as Lenovo, SAP, and Huawei have adopted such strategies. Take the case of Huawei, a Chinese technology company. For the last several years, the company has successfully used its key opinion leader (KOL) program to expand its global brand to new international markets. The KOL program includes more than one hundred influencers from many countries (e.g., the US, Canada, France), selected based on their influence in specific industry- or technology-focused communities that span different regions and countries. These influencers create digital content that relates to Huawei's different product categories (from VR to autonomous driving and IoT) and helps customers in foreign markets relate to those products and, importantly, to the underlying brand.

Companies can also involve their foreign market consumers in particular aspects of the global brand strategy, such as new product development and advertising campaigns (especially when IP policies and regulations are well aligned with global standards). Research has shown that the greater the involvement of consumers in such product- or brand-related value co-creation, the greater their loyalty and continued engagement with the brand.[17] Perhaps no company has used this as extensively and with as much impact as a Danish toy production company, the Lego Group. The company established its own digital platform to invite design ideas from customers across the world and to allow them to rate each idea, in the process not only enriching its product development pipeline but also fortifying the Lego global brand.

Importantly, a digital globalness strategy involves deploying standardized global digital assets—from global digital platforms to digitized processes to global influencers. The tight coupling that results from the application of such assets allows for high responsiveness (e.g., a new brand initiative can be launched rapidly across different foreign markets) but limited distinctiveness vis-à-vis specific foreign markets. When nationalistic and regional themes render consumer sentiments in a foreign market less inviting to global brands—making the local consumer culture distinctly different from the global consumer culture—such global branding efforts are less effective (and sometimes even detrimental). In such markets, the primary objective should be to imbue the brand with associations of local values, heritage, and authenticity so that consumers in the foreign market can identify with the local interpretation of the global brand.[18]

A digital culturation strategy, meanwhile, involves reinterpretation of a global brand in regional or local terms and implies loose coupling between the global brand and the local branding initiatives in a foreign market. Thus, the loose coupling used here is interpretive in nature: the global brand is reinterpreted, thereby bridging the divide between the global brand and the local consumer culture. This allows for maintaining local distinctiveness without endangering the company's ability to respond to changing market conditions.

Multinationals can accomplish this in two ways. First, new AI and big data analytics technologies can be used to identify relevant local cultural ideas and concepts in a market that align with a company's global brand. For example, machine learning can be used to mine local cultural data artifacts (song lyrics, movie dialog, books in various languages, etc.) at scale to tease out a key idea that could then be used for innovation and communication. Unilever, the $57 billion consumer goods multinational, has been pursuing such an approach for the last few years. Stan Sthanunathan, the company's executive vice president of consumer and market insights, has been the key force behind those efforts. As Stan told us, "AI and machine learning now allow us to develop critical insights, the big idea, that can transform how you communicate your brand in a specific market . . . in a way that is culturally meaningful or understandable to your customer there."[19] For example, Unilever's effort in this regard has involved mining songs and film dialog from Bollywood (India's Mumbai-based film industry) to unearth interesting metaphors, emerging trends, and key ideas rooted in the local culture and society that could be used in brand communication. Such efforts can also give rise to new product ideas; for example, the connection between ice cream and breakfast deciphered from several songs led to the creation of new breakfast flavors for Unilever's Ben & Jerry's ice cream brand.

The second way multinationals can maintain distinctiveness without loss of flexibility is to identify local influencers who can help reinterpret the global brand in terms of the local consumer culture and bring it closer to the customers in a foreign market. A wide range of multinationals, including Adidas, Lululemon, Google, Calvin Klein, Nike, Starbucks, Burberry, Ritz-Carlton, Unilever, and Adobe have pursued such an approach. For example, Burberry has used a local influencer in China—Mr. Bags, a.k.a. Tao Liang, a fashion guru with more than nine million followers—to launch new lines of leather bags. The strategy has enabled the company to reinterpret its brand in ways that resonate extremely well with Chinese customers. The reach and effectiveness of such strategies has also been quite evident; for example, in July 2020, a limited edition of a new pocket bag was sold out in exactly one minute. Importantly, the new leather bag was available only on Mr. Bags's WeChat; it wasn't even available on Burberry's own platforms.

Lululemon has built local WeChat groups as part of its community-building strategy in China, and this has allowed the company to go beyond individual influencers and make local *microinfluencer* groups to communicate the brand to the broader community of consumers. As Harish Bijoor, a brand-strategy consultant, noted, "In India, the use of local micro-influencers has aligned well with the rising 'vocal about local' movement or what I call the #DesiRevival movement and has enabled many foreign multinationals to develop a more locally imprinted storyline for their brands."[20] The trick here is to connect the brand's story with some key elements of the local culture that the microinfluencer (typically someone with fewer than fifty thousand followers on social media) represents/amplifies and to be authentic about it, which in turn calls for considerable care in selecting the microinfluencers. Unilever has started using AI technologies to make its search process for such microinfluencers faster and more effective. AI is now used not only to preselect influencers based on a number of demographic and cultural factors but also to detect those with fake followers.

Along with local influencers, the use of regional digital platforms also allows for a greater level of discretion for local brand managers with regard to how to engage with customers in a foreign market. For example, data privacy regulations that apply in a specific market may be better adhered to through the use of regional digital platforms. Further, the use of regional digital platforms, while enhancing the penetration in a foreign market, may enable a company to also limit the potential negative effects of poorly designed or executed brand initiatives. *Marketing crises*—broadly defined as publicized negative events stemming from marketing mix–related activities—can be disastrous for any company (e.g., product-harm scandals, false advertising, poorly sourced product ingredients, and unethical distribution practices).[21] Such crises can destroy carefully nurtured brand equity and cause major revenue and market-share losses. Because these negative effects are accentuated by the global reach of digital platforms, highly local or regional digital platforms and loose coupling between the global and the local brand may serve to limit such effects to a certain extent.

Digital globalness and digital culturation strategies indicate two contrasting ways for using digital technologies for brand-related engagement with customers in various foreign markets. Importantly, they incorporate different parameters—the use of global or local influencers, the nature and extent of the connection with local cultural artifacts, and the use of global or regional digital platforms and infrastructures. By considering these parameters carefully, companies can also develop strategies that represent different flavors of the digital globalness and culturation strategies. For example, consider the strategy that BMW adopted to market its new model of SUV in China. The company wanted to retain its global brand identity but decided that its global digital platform enjoyed limited visibility in the country. So the company created a virtual car show on Tencent's various regional social platforms and featured its stable of global influencers. Some ten million people viewed the show, which in turn helped the company create rapid awareness of its new model in China and at the same emphasized the global brand.

Conclusion

We started this chapter with a question: How are globalization and localization forces shaping multinational companies' market entry and customer connection strategies, and how are these strategies being redefined by digital technologies and platforms?

Our answer incorporates two sets of prototypical strategies:

1. *Global channel integration* and *digital-first*, which relate to a multinational's approach to entering and establishing its sales operations in a foreign market

2. *Digital globalness* and *digital culturation*, which relate to the company's approach to connecting its global brand with international customers

Our discussion also revealed the importance of carefully analyzing the underlying parameters—whether the extent of integration between digital and physical channels or the nature of connection with local cultural artifacts—to realize strategies that offer the optimal degree of tight coupling or loose coupling demanded by the foreign market context.

Although it is clear that multinationals can thus adapt their global customer and market strategies digitally based on the nature and intensity of the local/regional forces operative in a foreign market, most multinationals operate in a wide range of foreign markets—some that are highly globalized and others less so. A critical challenge then is to ensure that the overall customer strategy is coherent across different regions and markets. Lack of such coherence in marketing activities and brand messaging could sow confusion in consumers' minds.

The first step toward developing such coherence should be to understand the dimensions along which localization is allowed—for both sales operations (channels) and branding. Specifically, as we noted earlier, a foreign market may be distinct from the company's more globalized markets along three key dimensions: government policies/regulations and other institutional influences; the nature of local infrastructure (physical and digital); and consumer value systems and behaviors. Companies should craft broader strategies related to each of these. For example, what should the company's approach be if there is considerable disparity between its global digital platforms and the regional digital infrastructure in a market? If a common approach is employed across different foreign markets to adapt to such infrastructure-related disparities, there will be a greater level of consistency. In other words, though loose coupling can help multinationals retain distinctiveness when localization forces are high, there should also be consistency in how such loose coupling is applied in different foreign markets. This can allow for better orchestration of the company's customer connectivity strategies and resources across the world. We will return to this issue of consistency in chapter 10.

Next, we consider the second dimension of digital global business connectivity: connectivity with global partners, platforms, and ecosystems.

4 Connecting with Global Partners, Platforms, and Ecosystems Digitally

Yelp, founded in San Francisco in 2004, is known for its crowd-sourced reviews about local restaurants and businesses. While the company has found considerable success at home, it has struggled over the years to gain traction outside the United States and Canada. Starting around 2010, Yelp made considerable attempts to expand its operations in Europe, Asia, and South America. In Europe, the company pursued an expansion strategy by acquiring German-based restaurant review site Restaurant-Kritik and French-based Cityvox. Yelp also launched websites in countries such as Mexico, Japan, and Argentina. By 2013, its international revenues had climbed to about 4.6 percent of its overall business. However, overseas success didn't last long. By 2015, international revenues had fallen to 2.2 percent; by 2016, it was 1 percent. The company had fewer than five hundred international advertisers (who contributed about $2 million in revenue). And so, on November 2, 2016, Yelp announced it would drastically scale back its operations outside North America and effectively halt international expansion.

So what derailed Yelp's international expansion plans?

The short answer is digital platform dependency. Yelp was increasingly dependent on the Google search platform algorithms for driving its viewers. In the domestic market, it could balance this dependency with its own rich proprietary content (internal assets), but in most international markets, the company had less content and faced more competitors, making it particularly vulnerable to the vicissitudes of

Google's search platform. For example, when Google started to give less prominence to "organic" search results (the ones spit out by its algorithm) and more to the "vertical" results (the ones that Google provides based on its own data), Yelp started getting a lower number of hits on its offerings (reviews and ratings).[1] As the company noted in 2016, its inability to "achieve prominent display of our content in international unpaid search results disrupted the network effect we expected in our international markets based on what we experienced domestically, whereby increases in content led to increases in traffic."[2]

Yelp's travails in international markets underline two important issues that form the focus of this chapter. First, there is increasing awareness among new and established companies that their future depends not only what they do internally but also on how they connect with diverse sets of partners and collaborate in creating and delivering value to customers. Digital platforms and ecosystems that facilitate such value cocreation thus assume increasing significance in international expansion. At the same time, the relationships and associated dependencies that exist in such business ecosystems can radically alter a company's international prospects, as evidenced in the case of Yelp. Further, some of the key assumptions that underlie such platforms and ecosystems— for example, the relevance of the platform's focal value proposition in different markets, easy transfer of data and digital assets across borders, and shared goals among ecosystem members—are increasingly questioned by rising localization forces. As such, a multinational's continued success in foreign markets will require it to not only understand and manage the dependencies created by digital platforms and ecosystems but also to adapt its strategies to accommodate the diverse set of local and regional forces at play in different international markets.

Thus, in this chapter, we explore two questions: How are digital platforms and business ecosystems redefining multinational companies' international expansion strategies? And how should these platform and ecosystem strategies adapt to the globalization and localization forces at play in different foreign markets?

Before we address these questions, let's expand further on the three key trends that together indicate the relevance and importance of these questions.

First, no industry is now immune to the influence of digital platforms and ecosystems. The relentless waves of digitization that we have seen in many industries mean that companies have to view their offerings not just as standalone entities but also as part of a broader connected system. And increasingly these offerings comprise digital assets that can be easily transported across national and organizational boundaries and changed and recombined in different ways to cater to the needs of a particular foreign market. All of this increases the relevance of digital platforms and ecosystems beyond the usual suspects (e.g., consumer electronics, enterprise software) and into a wide range of other industries (including auto, power/utilities, health, education, and manufacturing).

Second, data forms the most valuable asset of a multinational these days (data begets intelligence) and lies at the core of its digital platform and ecosystem strategy. And when a platform has global reach, the key assumption is that such data can be moved around national borders to generate additional value. Increasingly, that assumption is being questioned as governments in almost all parts of the world develop policies and regulations that limit how/when/to what extent companies can transfer data across their borders (even within a company, from a subsidiary in one country to the corporate office in another country). Some data policies have been created to protect consumer rights (e.g., the EU's GDPR regulations or Russia's Federal Law 242-FZ), but other policies are related to an individual country's interest in protecting tax revenues from sales on global digital platforms (e.g., France's digital services tax). Whatever the motivation, such localized barriers to data flows will require companies to adopt appropriate regional platform strategies that can allow them to still enjoy benefits from their platforms and ecosystems.

Third, platforms and ecosystems derive much of their value from the size of their user base. On the one hand, a large user base that spans the world can considerably enhance the market power (and profits) of a multinational. Examples of this abound in both consumer-facing platforms (e.g., Facebook, Airbnb) and business-facing platforms (e.g., Alibaba). At the same time, such a global user base also indicates critical underlying dependencies related to regional and local forces. For example, take the case of Chinese platform companies such as ByteDance (which owns TikTok) and Tencent (which owns WeChat). Both TikTok and WeChat enjoy considerable market share in India, with approximately 30 percent of the global users of TikTok from India. However, recent tensions between India and China have highlighted how much the company's growth in India is predicated on bilateral relations. As a consequence of the ongoing tension between the two countries, India banned the use of about fifty apps, including TikTok and WeChat.[3] As relations improve in the future, the ban may be removed—but such actions indicate the unpredictability and impact of localization forces on a multinational's growth and performance in international markets.

All of these details imply that companies' strategies for orchestrating and participating in global platforms and ecosystems should factor in the unique aspects of the foreign markets they operate in—specifically, to what extent they are globalized or localized. Next, we identify design elements that are key to exploring this further.

Elements of Tight and Loose Coupling with Global Platforms and Ecosystems

We define two elements of a company's digital global business connectivity with regard to digital platforms and business ecosystems: platform-market connectivity and company-ecosystem connectivity.

The first element, *platform-market connectivity*, relates to how a company's digitized business platform connects with a foreign market in terms of its value proposition, digital assets, and data infrastructure. A company's platform can focus on applying the same focal value proposition and digital assets across different foreign markets, or it can specialize both its value proposition and digital assets to adapt to regional/ local policies and market needs—in effect, choosing between a global and a regional platform strategy. At the same time, such a platform can be embedded in a global data infrastructure or a regional data infrastructure. As we discuss in more detail in the next section, the different combinations of these choices give rise to alternate approaches or strategies that companies can calibrate to fit the extent of globalization and localization evident in different international markets, allowing for varying degrees of tight and loose coupling.

The second element, *company-ecosystem connectivity*, relates to how a company manages its relationships with its partners in different foreign markets and orchestrates value creation in the business ecosystem. We consider two key aspects here—the company's scope of engagement with its ecosystem partners in a foreign market and the nature of control and coordination it exercises in the ecosystem. Based on these two factors, we consider strategies or approaches that translate into tight and loose coupling in company-ecosystem connectivity.

In each of these elements, tight coupling represents greater levels of standardization in terms of the value proposed by the platform and how digital/data assets are deployed in an international market to realize it, as well as higher levels of a company's engagement, interaction, and coordination with international partners. All of these can enhance the overall responsiveness of the platform/ecosystem at the global level, but at the cost of losing its distinctiveness in the local market. On the other hand, loose coupling approaches—characterized by variants of the focal value proposition and digital assets, along with more localized areas of partner engagement—allow a multinational's platforms and ecosystems to better reflect and adapt to local conditions (i.e., to have more distinctiveness).

Let's consider these two elements in more detail now.

Platform-Market Connectivity and Digital Asset Deployment in Foreign Markets

Digital Assets and Digital Infrastructures

When companies expand to foreign markets, their primary goal is to deploy their unique internal or firm-specific advantages or assets in those markets to generate revenue. Often, companies may need to combine such firm-specific assets with those of a partner in a foreign market to create value and cater to local market needs. Digitization has converted many of these firm-specific assets into digital assets that are easily portable, modifiable, and combinable. In other words, compared to nondigital firm-specific assets such as reputation in a company's home country, digital firm-specific assets can be more readily moved across national borders, modified, and combined with those of a partner. Platforms provide a structure and venue for doing all this.

Of course, key choices for companies as they enter a foreign market include what digital assets they want to move to that market and how much to change those assets and/or combine them with partner assets. All of these decisions must take into consideration the features of the foreign market, including the relevance of the company's core value proposition and the prevailing national policies and regulations related to the transfer and use of foreign digital assets.

At the same time, digital platforms don't operate in a vacuum. They are dependent on the nature and quality of the digital infrastructure that is needed for the deployment of the digital assets and for customers to access those assets. As we discussed in chapter 2, there is considerable variation across countries in digital infrastructures. In some countries, such as those in the EU, digital infrastructures adhere to global standards, whereas in other countries, like China, they may be more closed and regional. Thus, as companies explore opportunities to expand the reach of their offerings, another key consideration is how their platforms will be embedded in the local or regional digital infrastructure. The more embedded the platform is in the local digital infrastructure, the more inroads the company can potentially make into a foreign market. However, this might also limit the extent to which the digital assets, including data, may be moved back and forth between the company's home country and the foreign market.

Thus, in the context of platforms, digital assets and digital infrastructures set up critical choices for companies in foreign markets. Should the company stick to a common global platform (one that involves minimal changes to the company's digital firm-specific assets), or should it deploy a regional platform that incorporates modified digital firm-specific assets? Should the company remain wedded to the global digital infrastructure, or should it align its platform more closely with the peculiarities of the regional digital infrastructure? As we discuss next, the choices a company makes in all of these areas will determine how tightly or loosely the company's platform is connected with a foreign market.

Tight and Loose Coupling in Platform-Market Connectivity

We consider two broad approaches or strategies in platform-market connectivity that are contingent on the nature and extent of localization forces: a global platform strategy and a regional platform strategy (see table 4.1).

Let's start with the *global platform strategy*, which involves deployment of a multinational's global digital assets embedded in a global digital infrastructure. This implies both the relevance of the platform's core value proposition and the prevalence of globalized data and digital infrastructures, policies, and regulations in the foreign market.

Take the case of Etsy. The US company, based in Brooklyn, New York, launched in 2005 and offers a digital platform that provides a global marketplace for handmade and vintage items and craft supplies. Etsy has about 4.3 million sellers around the world who produce over sixty

Table 4.1

Strategies for platform-market connectivity

| Strategy | Intensity of localization forces | | | |
	Government regulations and policies	Digital infrastructure	Business culture	Nature of coupling
Global platform	Low	Low	Low to moderate	Tight coupling
Regional platform	Moderate to high	Moderate to high	High	Loose coupling

million unique items annually for around eighty-two million buyers. Close to 40 percent of the company's over $1 billion revenue comes from international operations.

Etsy's platform is available in many countries around the world, but the company has largely focused on deploying a global platform with very little variation across the different markets. To a certain extent, this is reflective of the fact that the majority of its revenue comes from six countries: the United States, Canada, Germany, the UK, France, and Italy. As the company's chief technology officer, Mike Fisher, told us, "[Etsy] is focused on the big six markets. Everywhere else, it is on auto mode with limited investments."[4]

Because the "big six" markets happen to be in fairly globalized environments, the company can afford to deploy its digital platform and assets with limited accommodations made to fit local conditions. The platform's core value proposition retains relevance in all these markets, so there is limited need to modify the company's digital firm-specific assets. The company does have partners in some countries that write applications using Etsy's open application programming interfaces (APIs). But by and large, these partner apps are targeted at the needs of sellers in specific countries. For example, in some countries, Etsy's sellers employ multiple channels to reach their customers, so the partner apps help them to sync their inventory across these different channels. Similarly, in some other countries, such apps provide language translation services. However, the overall components and functions of Etsy's platform remain the same across different foreign markets. Further, the company relies on a common global digital infrastructure to operate its platform. Again, all of the six big markets adhere to similar digital infrastructure standards and technologies, and this allows the company to adopt a common strategy.

As Fisher noted, such a global platform strategy "has so far allowed us [Etsy] to limit our foreign investments and keep our operations lean."[5] In effect, it has enabled Etsy to enhance its overall efficiency and responsiveness without significantly sacrificing international sales. However, as the company expands to new markets in Asia and South

America that demand more distinctiveness, the company may need to revisit its platform strategy.

For example, the company recently started focusing on the vast market in India. Indian sellers had been on the Etsy platform since about 2013, but the company never had an office in India. That changed in 2018. Etsy set up its India operations that year but decided to focus only on Indian sellers rather than on both Indian sellers and buyers. There was a reason for this. The company still deployed its global platform as is (as it has done in EU countries) and viewed India as an export country. So the global platform and the company's digital firm-specific assets could still be applied without much change because Indian products would be primarily purchased by customers in the big six markets. As Himanshu Wardhan, who heads Etsy's India operations, told us, the company "did make a few accommodations based on the local digital infrastructure."[6] For example, the company's operations require sellers to register themselves via a desktop, but most Indian sellers have access to mobile phones and not to desktops or laptops. So Etsy's India office deployed a large contingent of associates who would physically go to sellers' locations across the country and sign them up.

All of these adaptations are fine if the focus remains only on Indian sellers. But if Etsy is interested in Indian buyers, it might need to rethink its platform strategy. The Indian e-commerce market is growing rapidly and is projected to reach about $91 billion by 2023.[7] So the opportunity to target Indian buyers is huge. At the same time, there are localization forces that the company will need to consider carefully. For example, certain aspects of the Indian digital infrastructure are different from those Etsy has faced in its existing markets, such as the quality of the digital connectivity beyond the larger and mid-sized cities. Similarly, Indian buyers' e-commerce behaviors are also different in certain respects, such as payment preferences. All of this might mean the need to depart from its reliance on global digital assets and to localize its platform to greater extent, at least with regard to its India initiative.

Indeed, as a company enters foreign markets that are more fragmented and subject to intense local/regional forces, the *regional platform strategy* assumes more salience. Such a strategy involves adapting the multinational's digital firm-specific assets to fit the foreign market conditions and/or embedding the digital firm-specific assets in the regional/local digital infrastructure. We will discuss two examples that illustrate when and how the regional platform strategy can be practiced.

Consider a scenario in which there are moderate amounts of local and regional forces at play. For example, maybe data policies or digital infrastructures are localized, but trade policies and business practices are not. In such a scenario, a company's global platform and digital assets may still largely be applicable, but accommodations may need to be made to adapt to local data/digital infrastructure and policies.

Mumbai-based Indian conglomerate Aditya Birla Group's digital platform initiative is illustrative in this regard. As we noted in chapter 2, ABG operates in over thirty countries, with more than 50 percent of its revenue coming from international operations. In recent years, the company has made considerable investments in building a robust, highly scalable, and portable platform that digitizes its operational processes and assets (for managing its machinery and operations in factories and other units across different geographical regions). Given the conglomerate's considerable presence in manufacturing sectors such as cement, metals, textiles, and chemicals, its preliminary emphasis has been on building a global portfolio of digital assets and platforms for these businesses to enable operational efficiencies and business performance.

The AI- and data analytics–based platform digitizes and modularizes several aspects of its operations, particularly interactions between different physical assets (machinery and other equipment) on the production floor and interactions between physical assets and human assets. The company is also working on making the digital platform outward-facing by allowing its global partners to connect with these digital assets in different ways. As Deep Thomas of ABG told us, "Our guiding goal has been to develop digital and AI-led platforms upon which we can build, deploy, and scale diverse solutions and use cases for our various divisions that could then be adapted to any of our business domains in any country of operation without changing the core functionality."[8]

In countries or regions where data policies and other digital infrastructure regulations are more restrictive, a company's digital platform assets could still be deployed with limited changes, albeit embedded more tightly with the local digital infrastructure. This is the strategy that ABG has adopted in places such as the EU, where there are specific data privacy and security policies at play. For example, one platform employs AI, computer vision, and facial-recognition technologies to monitor oil spillage, people's movements in unsafe work zones, and other safety-related events.[9] When such interactions are anonymized, the digital assets can be ported across the company's different businesses in different countries. And even when the interactions involve identifying information about people, the same digital assets can be deployed, albeit walled in by the regional digital infrastructure. All of this implies enhancing the platform's distinctiveness with regard to the local infrastructure and conditions.

When there are significant differences in government data policies/regulations and in the digital infrastructure, companies may need to carefully pick and choose what elements of their global digital assets are relevant and rebuild the platform for the foreign market; in essence, they will need to create a regional platform more attuned to the local conditions.

Bayer's ongoing initiative in India is illustrative of this. Bayer AG, a German multinational pharmaceutical and life sciences company, recently acquired the US-based biotech company Monsanto, a leading producer of genetically engineered crops, for $63 billion. With that acquisition came the agriculture industry's leading digital farming platform, Climate FieldView.[10] The platform offers a bevy of digital tools for farmers to easily collect and store data on their operations year-round and to optimize their decisions quickly and efficiently, thereby helping them reach their yield potential while minimizing application of crop inputs. The platform, launched in 2018, has been deployed in diverse markets, including in at least fifteen EU countries, as well as in Argentina and Brazil.

However, FieldView is primarily suited for farmers holding considerable farm acreage. In India, that is not the case. Most Indian farmers are subsistence farmers or smallholder farmers who farm on less than two acres of land and hence cannot afford (or even need) sophisticated digital platforms. Further, the Indian digital infrastructure is still evolving, and local farmers are largely reliant on low-end smartphones as their primary digital tool (with high-latency internet connectivity). Although the Indian government has adopted several measures to promote digital agriculture, there are still regulations and policies—related to both agriculture and to data security and privacy—that present additional sets of challenges.

All of these present a case for localization, so Bayer has pursued an initiative to reinvent its digital platform for the Indian market. As D. Narian, vice chairman and managing director of Bayer Crop Science, told us, "It is clear that digital tools are going to revolutionize farming in India too. However, what all of us need to figure out is what are the key pain points for the Indian farmer and how can we introduce specific layers and components of our digital platform in ways that would deliver value . . . and that is the journey that we are now on."[11]

Specifically, the company is drawing on the capabilities of its FieldView global platform, but reimagining those capabilities for small farmers. To this end, the company has assembled a team in India to develop and start testing models. FarmRise is an Android-based app that reflects the architecture and learnings from FieldView and at the same time, includes new digital assets developed for the Indian context, as well as assets contributed by ecosystem partners in India.[12] The app offers agronomic information and advice relevant to smallholder farmers (e.g., local/regional commodity market prices, information about agriculture-related Indian government schemes, and crop-specific advice), allowing them to make decisions that fit with their particular local context. As Narian notes, "Obviously the backbone for that comes from Climate, but at the same time, we have an ecosystem with multiple startups in

India and we enable others to plug in to our emerging solution . . . so that's the way we will build this." Thus, the broader goal of Bayer India is to localize the company's global digital platform capabilities to adapt to the unique market, regulatory, and infrastructural issues presented by the Indian agricultural context.

Such a regional platform strategy represents a loose coupling that enhances a platform's distinctiveness in a foreign market without losing its responsiveness (vis-à-vis the multinational's global platform). The responsiveness may be based on the common or shared architecture or some core assets, but the distinctiveness is derived from the localized digital assets and/or its embedding in local digital infrastructures. As table 4.1 shows, such a strategy assumes particular relevance in foreign markets that are characterized by localized policies and regulations related to data, industry, or infrastructure.

Company-Ecosystem Connectivity

A multinational's connection with its business ecosystem and foreign partners also needs to be designed based on the intensity of local and regional forces. Two important aspects of such ecosystem-based relationships are the company's scope of engagement with its global partners and the nature of control and coordination it deploys in the ecosystem. We suggest two broad strategies that incorporate these two factors: digital embrace and digital handshake (see table 4.2).

The *digital embrace* strategy implies a broad scope of engagement with ecosystem partners in value creation (from innovation to operations) and a close level of digitally enabled coordination in various value-creation activities, largely based on shared goals and shared values. Such an approach involves a greater level of sharing of digital and other assets with partners and coordinating activities that relate to modifying and recombining those assets in myriad ways to generate value in different market contexts. However, such broadened and close engagement with foreign partners also establishes a greater extent of interdependencies. In turn, this demands a common set of rules and

Table 4.2
Strategies for company-ecosystem connectivity

| Strategy | Intensity of regional/local forces | | | |
	Government regulations and policies	Digital infrastructure	Business culture	Nature of coupling
Digital embrace	Low	Low to moderate	Low	Tight coupling
Digital handshake	Moderate to high	High	Moderate to high	Loose coupling

policies so as to minimize opportunities for one partner to derive undue advantage and to lower the overall uncertainty in the collaborative activities. Further, when there is sufficient overlap in the regulation/policies and business culture between a company's home market and the foreign market, it becomes possible for the company to adopt more direct coordination practices. Thus, typically market contexts that are more globalized present more suitable environments for multinationals to digitally embrace their ecosystem partners.

On the other hand, when local and regional considerations assume greater significance in a foreign market, it may become more difficult for a multinational and its foreign partners to find such a common ground—leading to narrower scope of engagement, with more emphasis placed on digital monitoring than on digital coordination, which we call the *digital handshake* strategy. In other words, compared to the digital embrace strategy, which reflects a digitally enabled, collaborative approach, the digital handshake strategy reflects a digitally enabled, arm's-length or transactional relationship. For example, disparities in IP-related policies between a company's home country and a foreign market may present a critical challenge to deeply engage with partners in innovation. When the "who owns what" question cannot be clearly answered, companies may feel the need to narrow their areas of direct engagement. Similarly, disparities in business culture (between the multinational's home country and the foreign market) may limit the adoption of shared ecosystem-level values and norms and force multinationals to pursue tightly defined and narrow (transactional) engagement with foreign partners, wall off their decision-making processes, and transition from coordination of to monitoring (by enhancing the digital visibility) partner activities.

Consider how Philips Healthcare has developed its ecosystem in the United States and Canada.[13] The Dutch multinational conglomerate corporation, headquartered in Amsterdam, offers a digital connected health platform called HealthSuite that provides a host of cloud-based capabilities to connect multiple medical devices, collect electronic health data, aggregate and securely analyze data, and create solutions in the cloud. To enhance the reach and range of its platform, Philips has started building an ecosystem of partners, including other healthcare providers (hospitals), medical device companies, and technology companies, largely focused on the North American market. And in doing so, the company's dominant approach has been the digital embrace strategy.

The company has entered into long-term, shared goals and values-driven close partnership with a host of healthcare providers, including Phoenix Children's hospital, Banner Health, and Marin General Hospital. For example, its partnership with Canada-based Mackenzie Health involves serving "as a core innovation partner that will supply future-forward solutions for smart hospital and extended community of care."[14] Similarly, it has forged close partnerships with several technology companies (including enterprise computing companies) to further enhance the value delivered by the ecosystem. For example, Philips partnered with Validic, a US-based digital health platform, to bring consumer-generated data from third-party devices (e.g., fitness wearables, remote monitoring devices, and health apps) into Philips's HealthSuite to be integrated and analyzed in conjunction with a patient's electronic medical record and other clinical data sources. With these and other such ecosystem members, partnership agreements involve significant sharing and integration of digital and data assets in ways that enhance the value of Philips's platform.

The company has followed such a digital embrace strategy outside North America too. For example, in South Korea, Philips has partnered with Samsung so that they can use one another's digital assets and platforms.[15] Specifically, the two companies will integrate their individual platforms and ecosystems—Samsung's ARTIK Smart IoT platform and Philip's HealthSuite platform—to realize interoperable connected health solutions using integrated data sets and services such as advanced health analytics.

In China, the company has pursued a different approach, one marked by a narrower set of engagements with partners. Philips has set up an innovation hub (R&D center) in Shanghai, but its partnerships with leading Chinese technology companies are all largely infrastructural in nature. For example, it has partnered with Huawei to use its cloud AI platform to deploy Philips's offerings. Similarly, it has partnered with BAT (Baidu, Alibaba, Tencent) to avail itself of different types of digital infrastructures that can extend the reach and scope of Philips's core offerings in China. The company is pursuing certain innovation projects with some of these Chinese companies (e.g., developing AI-based solutions with Huawei), but they are limited in scope and largely aim to serve the Chinese market. Importantly, they involve very limited sharing of digital assets and other IP with partners.

Bayer's ecosystem strategy in India is illustrative of a mix of these two prototypical strategies. As we noted earlier, the company has embarked on a project to develop a localized digital platform for Indian farmers. In parallel, the company has also started building its ecosystem to support its digital initiatives in India. In 2018, Bayer formed the Better Life Farming alliance, which brought together global and local partners across the agriculture value chain to help smallholder farmers unlock their farming potential. In India, the Better Life Farming alliance is led by Bayer and a host of other organizations, including International Finance Corporation (a member of the World Bank Group), Netafim, Yara, DeHaat, and Big Basket.

Bayer's digital platform and capabilities form a key ingredient of this alliance, but the company's engagement with ecosystem partners falls somewhere in between the digital embrace and digital handshake strategies. For example, Bayer partnered with Agribazaar, an Indian agritech platform that provides an online marketplace for smallholder farmers. On the one hand, the partnership involves an arm's-length linkage that will allow the farmers under Bayer's Better Life Farming initiative get better prices for their produce via the Agribazaar platform. At the same time, Bayer has established a closer relationship with Agribazaar, involving integration of its individual platform services, allowing Bayer to extend the reach of its crop advisory services to a larger set of farmers on the Agribazaar marketplace. Similarly, Bayer has also partnered with Indian conglomerate ITC's agribusiness division to extend the reach of its crop protection products through ITC's e-Choupal 4.0 digital platform.

More broadly, these examples illustrate the two archetypes of company-ecosystem connectivity and, importantly, the possibilities for middle ground strategies. Broader engagement and digitally enabled coordination imply frequent interactions, sharing of assets, and overall tighter coupling between a company and its ecosystem partners. The greater alignment of trade policies and regulations, digital infrastructures, and business cultures between the United States and Philips's home country enabled the company to pursue such a tighter coupling with its partners. At the same time, the need to adopt shared values, common rules, and policies may limit the number and diversity of its partners in a foreign market and thereby limit the local distinctiveness of the value created by its ecosystem. In China, however, the company faced distinctly different IP policies and business culture and more regional digital infrastructures, thereby demanding a looser coupling with partners that would allow for greater distinctiveness (localized digital platforms). The case of Bayer in India demonstrates a company's options for ecosystem connectivity when localization forces like regional digital infrastructures coexist with globalization forces like globalized IP policies.

Recall Yelp's international expansion problems in EU markets that arose from its dependency on Google's search algorithms. When a

multinational's growth in a foreign market is dependent on complementary assets owned by another company, it becomes even more critical to evaluate the nature and intensity of localization forces in that
market carefully and, based on that, to adopt an appropriate strategy.
As Yelp's case indicates, lack of such a context-based relationship could
significantly lower the value of the multinational's firm-specific assets
in that market and hinder its growth and fortunes there. Importantly,
in many foreign markets, the localization forces are dynamic; in turn,
this calls for companies to continually reevaluate the nature of connectivity in their ecosystems in different parts of the world.

Conclusion

We started this chapter with a question: How are digital platforms and
business ecosystems redefining multinational companies' international
expansion strategies, and how should their platform and ecosystem
strategies adapt to the globalization and localization forces at play in
different international markets?

Our answer here incorporates two sets of prototypical strategies:

1. *Global platform strategy* and *regional platform strategy*, which relate to
   how a multinational's digitized business platform connects with a
   foreign market in terms of its value proposition, digital assets, and
   data infrastructure

2. *Digital embrace* and *digital handshake*, which relate to how a multinational manages its relationships with its partners in different
   international markets and orchestrates value creation in the business
   ecosystem in those countries

Our discussion also revealed the need to carefully consider middle
ground strategies—those that incorporate marrying global digital assets
with regional infrastructure or limiting the scope of interactions and
engagement with a foreign partner to a specific set of value creation
activities, ones that offer the optimal degree of tight coupling or loose
coupling demanded by the foreign market context.

It is clear that multinationals can thus adapt their partner, platform, and ecosystem strategies to fit different foreign market conditions based on the nature and intensity of the localization forces, but it is also evident that most multinational companies operate in a wide range of foreign markets, some that are highly globalized and some less so. Further, some multinational companies may have multiple platforms that operate within a single foreign country but face different types of localization forces.

For example, Tencent, the Chinese multinational conglomerate, manages multiple platforms (each with its own separate ecosystem) in different industries and sectors—ranging from gaming and social media platforms to financial technology and IoT-based manufacturing platforms—and in different foreign markets. Tencent took years to orchestrate its multiple platforms because China's app-distribution ecosystem was very fragmented, with over two hundred marketplaces—but eventually, it successfully launched Tencent Open Platform in 2014. This integrated platform now enables three hundred million or so developers to rapidly attract millions of users from Tencent's huge user base by releasing applications via a range of platforms, such as Tencent App Store, Tencent QQ, WeChat, Qzone, and QQ Game. Yet the challenge remains for Tencent to ensure that its platform and ecosystem strategies are consistent across different industry and regional markets.

Adoption of ad hoc and conflicting strategies in different international markets could lead to considerable overhead costs (e.g., time and effort in resolving disputes with foreign partners) and lead to inconsistencies in how a multinational's platform creates and delivers value globally. There are two possible paths to address this. First, the framework that we offer here—specifically, the focus on three dimensions of the foreign market context: trade policies/regulations, infrastructure, and culture—could serve as the basis for companies to develop a more coherent, worldwide set of strategies. A multinational could devise and promote a consistent set of strategies across all its foreign subsidiaries to address similar issues related to a particular type of localization force—say, disparities in data security and privacy policies between the company's home country and a foreign market. Second, beyond using such frameworks to devise strategies, the different types of capabilities that companies bring to address issues related to inconsistencies across foreign markets are also equally important. We will return to this issue in chapter 10 as we examine employee-, business unit-, and organization-level capabilities that multinationals need to invest in to maintain such a holistic perspective of their digital global business connectivity.

Next, we consider how companies can manage their global operations and activities digitally.

5 Connecting with Foreign Subsidiaries and Managing Global Activities Digitally

A multinational enterprise consists of a group of geographically dispersed and often goal-disparate organizations that include headquarters and different subsidiaries abroad. Foreign subsidiaries are subject to the laws of the country in which they reside, as well as certain statutes of the nation in which the parent firm is domiciled. The multinational firm must thus differentiate its foreign subunits enough to successfully confront cultures, markets, and business practices that contrast markedly with those of the home country, but within a coherent structure in order to provide a maximum contribution to corporate performance.

The history of Unilever, the British-Dutch multinational consumer goods conglomerate that sells its products in more than 190 countries, is a good illustration of the dilemma that many multinational enterprises face with regard to a company's linkages with its foreign subsidiaries and their activities. For much of its early existence, Unilever's country subsidiaries were run independently, answerable to headquarters primarily in terms of financial goals and performance. There was limited integration of supply chains across the subsidiaries in different countries or, for that matter, integration of any other function. All of that changed starting in the early 1990s. There were growing calls for greater levels of global integration of operations across different subsidiaries. On the one hand, this was fueled by external pressures to reduce costs and enhance operational efficiencies. At the same time, increasing levels of digitization in different parts of the conglomerate made such integration feasible and even appealing. For the next twenty years or so, Unilever made significant investments to pursue global HR, global supply chains, global marketing, and global financial management initiatives. But a few years ago, the integration pendulum started swinging back as localization forces became ascendant in different parts of the world. For example, in Asia, there were renewed efforts to disaggregate some operations, allowing country subsidiaries or those within a region greater levels of leeway in marketing, logistics, and other functional areas.

This integration-disaggregation dilemma is not unique to Unilever. Most multinational enterprises today face a global business landscape that seems to pull them simultaneously in both directions. But global integration is necessary for several reasons.

Interunit sharing, learning, and resource flows require extensive coordination and careful organization within a company. To nurture this sharing, many multinationals assign different global mandates to different subsidiaries. For example, Siemens's subsidiary in Japan, in partnership with Asahi Intecc Medical, has a worldwide responsibility to produce compact magnetic resonance imaging (MRI) machines, while its peer subsidiary in Singapore has a worldwide responsibility to distribute and market these machines. To execute such globally interdependent operations, parent firms need efficient organizing and integrating mechanisms in place.

Financial management for global operations—such as executing transfer pricing (for reducing taxation or tariffs), global financing and equity participation, risk control and exposure management, and the use of an internal bank (for intracorporate financing, foreign exchange hedging, and cash flow management)—necessitates global coordination and integration. Increasing globalization of financial markets, along with digital global business connectivity, has fundamental implications for a multinational's corporate finance. In this environment, management's ability to seize opportunities and avoid unnecessary risks depends on its knowledge of the international environment and its financial management skills. To this end, global integration by corporate headquarters becomes imperative.

Similarly, heightened standards and needs for better governance, transparency, compliance, and sustainability compel international businesses to execute greater coordination and integration of worldwide activities. Indeed, the centerpiece of the design of global corporate compliance is augmenting the firm's ability to exert the necessary control over its foreign subsidiaries.

As with Unilever, in the last two decades, most multinational enterprises have been on a global integration spree based on the assumption that they can no longer afford to compete as a collection of independent subsidiaries. Forces related to economies of scale and technological developments have propelled many multinationals to integrate the value chain activities performed in their subsidiaries around the world Integrating these activities means raising the level of interdependence among subsidiaries, thus demanding global coordination. Indeed, competition has become based in part on the ability of companies to link their subsidiary activities across geographic locations in order to transform their supply chains into highly efficient, global, multistage production networks that can trim every remaining bit of fat from the system.

However, as localization forces become more acute in different parts of the world, the integration pendulum seems to be swinging back. Issues and concerns related to the sustainability of global supply chains and the negative effects of high levels of interdependencies among subsidiaries have been raised.[1] The COVID-19 pandemic and the ensuing disruptions in global value chains has further enhanced some of these concerns. There are new efforts ongoing in many multinationals to disaggregate, or at least regionalize, production, supply chains, innovation, and other activities.

Yet the need for global integration hasn't disappeared. In fact, there is still much to be gained from coordinating activities across regions and countries. And it is this challenging context—in which the need for both integration and disaggregation coexist—that forms the setting for the current chapter.

Specifically, here, we ask: How should multinationals navigate the emerging international business landscape that calls for both integration and disaggregation of their subsidiary operations/activities in order to respond to globalization and localization forces at play in different foreign markets? And importantly, how does digitization help in addressing this challenge?

As we discuss in detail ahead, a company's digital global business connectivity is central to resolving the integration/disaggregation dilemma. For example, digital technologies and infrastructure advances lead to offshoring and outsourcing of operations, thus increasing disaggregation of some value chain activities. At the same time, digitization also helps bring together such disaggregated activities unfolding in different countries and providing value-added total solutions critical for maintaining global competitiveness. What is important, however, is not necessarily the digital technologies per se or the associated strategies but how such digital global business connectivity is fashioned, considering the varying levels of globalization-localization forces.

Elements of Tight and Loose Coupling in Managing Global Activities

We define a company's digital global business connectivity with regard to managing its global operations and activities in terms of the company-subsidiary connectivity.

Company-subsidiary connectivity relates to a company's relationship with its subsidiaries in different countries and reflects the coordination processes and the allocation of decision-making powers. Companies often make distinct choices in this regard. One approach is to adopt an *intelligent hub model*, wherein significant decision-making powers are vested in the headquarters (or in regional hubs) and there is considerable integration and coordination of global activities across subsidiaries in different countries and regions. The alternate approach involves locating much of the intelligence and decision-making power at the edges of the company's global production and supply chain networks—in other words, with the subsidiaries and the frontline units. We call this the *intelligent edge model*. In such a model, the extent of integration and coordination is often limited to, at the most, a few subsidiaries within a region.

The intelligent hub and intelligent edge models offer distinct sets of advantages and disadvantages, reflecting those from integration and disaggregation, respectively. However, it is not these individual choices but their combination that give rise to effective strategies that companies can calibrate to fit the extent of globalization and localization, allowing for varying degrees of tight and loose coupling. And as we discuss in this chapter, such approaches are increasingly made feasible by advances in digital technologies such as IoT, digital sensors, AI, and blockchain.

Next, we first briefly describe the two models, and then discuss strategies that involve combining the two.

Intelligent Hubs and Intelligent Edges: Redefining Multinational Enterprise-Subsidiary Connectivity

From Global Supply Chains to Global HR: The Intelligent Hub Approach

Over the past two decades or so, the opportunity to realize gains from locating business activities in different parts of the world largely based on the cost structure has led to the intelligent hub model, wherein a few key global hubs of a multinational develop and control critical capabilities or resources and make them available and accessible for subsidiaries in other countries to use. Such an approach also reflects the realization that multinationals are no longer able to compete as a collection of independent subsidiaries. However, beyond such economic and competitive motives, the availability of powerful digital technologies has also been a key factor in moving toward such a model.

Digital connectivity allows global businesses to organize operations in ways that are fast, integrated, and streamlined. Connectivity not only makes intrafirm linkages easier but also, importantly, makes such linkages more productive and efficient. A company-wide common digital architecture and associated enterprise-wide systems can facilitate the management of dispersed operations and modularized activities performed in different countries.

For example, an integrated and highly scalable enterprise resource planning (ERP) solution, such as SAP Business One, allows global businesses to establish a tightly integrated global value chain and manage all types of cross-border flows in an orchestrated manner. Similarly, a global intranet accessible by all global employees signifies a great vehicle for developing automated business processes across an entire organization. It not only helps create global, virtual organizations with team members from different subsidiaries but also allows for access to existing office systems such as Google Apps for straightforward access by employees in different parts of the world.

Such digital business connectivity also allows multinationals to identify where, when, and what capabilities and resources should best be deployed and in a most productive way, thus helping to reconfigure, maneuver, and improve existing resources and capabilities for global operations. Space no longer constitutes an independent exogenous variable for companies. Rather, by stitching together geographically dispersed global resources and value chain activities, multinationals can pursue a truly global strategy.

Clearly, by cultivating such enterprise-wide integration and coordination of geographically dispersed activities, the intelligent hub model helps tame business complexity and create leaner organizations. It enables international businesses to achieve greater returns from integration, coordination, and collaboration between the corporate headquarters and foreign subsidiaries and among foreign subsidiaries in different locations. For example, in the early 2000s, Unilever pursued a significant restructuring of its supply chain management, which focused on establishing global procurement processes across its different subsidiaries and businesses. In the process, it achieved $14.24 billion in savings. Similarly, starting in 2011 or so, Cisco set about consolidating its multiple supply chain processes across the world and established a standardized end-to-end single global ERP instance for catering to the company's supply chain needs across its different businesses. This resulted in significant efficiency gains, including up to a 73 percent reduction in order cycle times, more than a 30 percent reduction in time to market, and a 30–50 percent reduction in support costs.

Such efficiency gains drove multinationals to pursue ever tighter global systems in all business functions—from supply chains and production to HR and marketing. Indeed, by the late 2000s, competition had become largely based on the ability of a multinational corporation to link its subsidiary activities across geographic borders and implement a coherent and tightly coordinated global hub–based business template. However, such continued optimization of global activities through digital technologies can also lead to a point at which the strategic and structural resilience of a multinational's global operations is questioned.

By 2015 or so, it was clear that strong localization forces that could derail multinationals' globally integrated operations were ascendant in many parts of the world. All of this came to a head in the last three to four years: the US-China trade conflict took hold, and Brexit and other events showed a world in which the relevance and value of the intelligent hub model was increasingly questionable. The COVID-19 crisis was perhaps the last straw that made multinationals sit up and question the trade-offs they were making in pursuing tightly integrated global operation systems, and it triggered a move in the opposite direction—toward the intelligent edge model.

A Shift to the Intelligent Edge Model: Response to the COVID-19 Crisis?

An event like the COVID-19 crisis or even the US-China trade conflict leads to a siloed world as borders become less permeable. A natural response is to incorporate greater leeway in individual subsidiary operations. The intelligent edge model reflects such an approach—disaggregating global activities to the extent that much of the operational planning and decision-making are conducted at the edges of a multinational's global network, where the subsidiaries reside.

Indeed, two important changes constituted multinational companies' response to the COVID-19 crisis. First, there has been an intentional shift away from global coordination to greater levels of regionalization, a recognition that configuring operations based only on global cost optimization is not sustainable in a world that can be easily disrupted and cannot always assure a globalized business landscape. Second, there has also been a radical shift toward greater digital connectivity in company operations. In a matter of days or weeks, companies massively stepped up their use of technologies to enable remote operations and delivery of offerings to customers. Digital business models and virtualized business operations have been proven to be plausible and scalable even in those industries that traditionally resisted such ways of conducting business. Successful companies during the pandemic were those that were quickly able to become digital-centric—using digital global business connectivity to quickly reorganize and reconfigure global operations.

Importantly, some companies had already started moving in the direction of the intelligent edge model by adopting greater levels of regionalization/localization in their operations. Toyota has practiced localization to a greater extent than many of its competitors; for example, for its Georgetown, Kentucky, factory, Toyota had located more than 350 suppliers in the United States and more than one hundred inside the state of Kentucky. Similarly, 3M moved to such a model in some of its operations: respirator masks and personal protective equipment (PPE) are manufactured in China for the Chinese market, in South Korea for the greater Asian market, and in the United States for the North American market.

Some companies also started moving away from the *just-in-time* methods that characterized intelligent hub operations to *just-in-case* scenarios that reflect greater localization of operations. For example, Master Kong, China's largest instant noodle company, learned its lesson from the earlier SARS crisis and built just-in-case capabilities (which involved continuous tracking of retail outlets' reopening plans, anticipating hoarding and stockouts, and dynamically shifting supply chain focus from large offline outlets to ecommerce and small retail outlets), allowing it to serve Chinese consumers in virtually every city and every province during the COVID-19 lockdowns and shelter-at-home orders.[2] Several companies have also moved toward enhancing the geographical diversity of their suppliers; although there are costs to adding alternative supply sources and increasing safety stocks, a key long-term benefit is greater supply chain resilience.

The intelligent edge model recognizes that when disruptive events occur, swift reconfiguration and mobilization of resources and rapid problem-solving require giving sufficient autonomy to subsidiaries on the front line. Indeed, one of the reasons that Haier, a Chinese multinational in the home appliances market, quickly rebounded from the COVID-19 crisis was its unique organizational structure, made of hundreds of self-managing business units (microenterprises) that make their own rapid adjustments to stay afloat in such times of crisis.[3]

Efficiency and Resilience: Combining Intelligent Hub and Intelligent Edge Models

While the intelligent edge approach addresses localization forces, the approach to addressing the globalization/localization dilemma should not simply be moving to the other end of the continuum—from global integration to global disaggregation. Rather, it is through a judicious mix of both models that multinationals will be able to achieve the best trade-off between efficiency and resilience in their operations.[4] *Resilience* is the ability to effectively cope with, recover from, or adapt to challenging or disruptive situations. To adapt to disruptive situations, a firm and its subsidiaries still need collaboration and coordination (and thus coupling), but at the same time, resilience also requires reduction of external dependence (and thus looseness). Such a combined approach therefore implies a loose coupling between a company and its subsidiaries that can be conditioned based on the extent of globalization and localization forces (see table 5.1).

Note that there still might be international market contexts in which such looseness is not at all required, in which case the tight coupling

Table 5.1
Strategies for company-subsidiary connectivity

	Intensity of localization forces			
Strategy	Government regulations and policies	Digital infrastructure	Business culture	Nature of coupling
Intelligent hub	Low	Low	Low	Tight coupling
Intelligent hub/ intelligent edge	Moderate to high	Moderate to high	Moderate to high	Loose coupling

inherent in the intelligent hub model may be not only appropriate but also desired (as table 5.1 shows). As we have already discussed the intelligent hub model, in the remainder of this chapter we will focus on the combination of the two models that implies loose coupling.

So, how does such a combined approach differ from the two individual models described earlier? Broadly, it involves having a number of global and regional hubs embedded in an overall structure that is less hierarchical, infused with strong orchestration capabilities, and constituting subsidiaries that enjoy greater levels of autonomy. Three key themes capture the essence of such an approach: reliance on a *global operations template* imparted by the hubs; differentiated levels of *autonomy* for subsidiaries in different countries and regions; and enterprise-wide *orchestration capabilities* that enhance the entire firm's dynamic capability to reconfigure operations and respond rapidly to demanding situations.

Global and regional hubs serve not only to leverage a multinational's resource advantage and market advantage and contribute to its worldwide reach but also, importantly, to offer a global vision or an operations template that could be quickly refashioned by its subsidiaries in different countries. To enable this, global hubs have to be situated in a flatter or less hierarchical structure that relies extensively on information linkages and rapid data flows within the company. Further, subsidiaries are empowered with more authority, enabling frontier units in key international markets to play a much bigger role in both global integration and local adaptation. Finally, orchestration capabilities are not just situated within global hubs but also infused throughout the company, including in all its subsidiaries, enabling them to reconfigure resources and activities locally and regionally when needed. *Orchestration capability* refers to a firm's ability to pursue an opportunity not by controlling all the required resources and competencies but by assembling, organizing, synthesizing, and integrating all globally available resources, including those from open markets, ecosystem partners, and the firm itself. Orchestration thus denounces the conventional boundaries of "host" and "home" countries for multinationals and instead views the global market as a networked, interconnected, and interdependent environment wherein capability and resource sharing from internal and external channels and across borders allows the firm to adapt rapidly to changing conditions.

Thus, both intelligent hub and intelligent edge models coexist, allowing a multinational to adapt quickly to changing globalization and localization forces. While the combination of global templates and orchestration capabilities allow companies to gain efficiencies in global operations when and where applicable, the same orchestration capabilities combined with decentralized horizontal flexibility helps build more resilience in operations.

Ahead, we illustrate three key aspects of this approach, with examples drawn from different industries. As our examples indicate, digital technologies and, importantly, data and analytics play a critical role in enabling all this; indeed, without digital global business connectivity, it would be unfeasible to adopt this approach.

Virtualization of business operations and digital twin strategy. *Virtualization* involves creating a virtual (software-based) representation of a business operation or activity. Such virtualization relates to all three themes identified earlier: it allows organizations to build global operations templates, enhances a firm's orchestration capabilities through simulations and data analysis, and enables subsidiaries to leverage their autonomy to adapt or modify global templates in order to rapidly respond to local disruptions.

A *digital twin* is simply a virtual model of a process, product, or service. By building a virtual model of a company's operations (production, supply chain) and then pairing that with real-world (physical) operations, companies can run simulations and analyze data to predict potential problems and develop alternative paths to resolve them. Digital technologies such as IoT, sensors, AI, and data analytics have made all of this feasible and also quite cost-effective.

For example, Unilever has built virtual versions of its factories, using data streaming from IoT sensor-equipped machines to create digital models that can track physical conditions and enable testing of operational changes, both locally and globally.[5] The company has eight such digital twins in plants in North America, South America, Europe, and Asia. In coming years, the company will also create virtual versions of dozens of its roughly three hundred global plants. This digital twin strategy has allowed Unilever to analyze big data from hundreds of connected devices using advanced analytics and machine-learning algorithms and make real-time changes to optimize output and reduce waste—making production more efficient and at the same time responsive to local changes.

The company also found that the algorithms can reach levels of accuracy at which they can be allowed to directly control part of a machine or process—not only enabling local managers to make better-informed decisions but also freeing them up for more value-added functions. For example, Unilever recently established its first completely lights-out supply chain operation in India, using real-time data and algorithms to make decisions that are then acted upon by robots operating in large warehouses. As Zaved Akhtar, who leads Unilever's digital transformation efforts in South Asia, told us, "Our ability to tap into multiple real-time data streams combined with analytics and automation now allow us to push intelligence to the very edge of our local operations, factories and distribution centers, and at the same time operate from a larger book of learnings on demand fulfillment derived from our operations across the enterprise."[6] The company aims to get gains from both worlds: virtual global models that inform the algorithms and real-time data analytics and simulations that adapt those algorithms to local conditions.

Similarly, both Nike and Johnson & Johnson used this kind of virtualization to respond to the disruptions caused to their supply chains by the COVID-19 pandemic crisis. Johnson & Johnson employed simulation and risk-analysis tools along with its supply chain virtualization to identify alternative paths for foreign supplies to its manufacturing plants.[7] Because China (one of the most affected countries in the early part of 2020) formed the company's major market, such operational flexibility was critical for the company to maintain continuity in its operations. Similarly, Nike employed its digital and data analytics capabilities along with the operational inputs from its foreign subsidiary executives and local teams to run different scenarios. Based on that, it optimized its foreign production plans and rerouted products from physical stores to e-commerce sales.[8]

In these and other examples, virtualization of operations becomes a key vehicle for a multinational's global hubs to build a global operations template that can optimize efficiency and communicate that to all subsidiaries. At the same time, a virtualization strategy also enables individual subsidiaries to adapt operations templates based on simulations and analysis using real-time data. Importantly, the scope of such simulations and data analysis can be global or local—implying how the orchestration capabilities needed to rapidly reconfigure resources/ activities are infused throughout the firm.

Virtualization of skills and virtual talent marketplaces. In chapter 1, we briefly mentioned how digitization has allowed companies to tap into a vast global network of resources outside their organizational boundaries. For example, digital connectivity allows multinationals to tap global freelancers who are experts in the areas in which the firms do not have any or enough talent. Using such freelance talent can be cheaper, faster, more flexible, and easier to manage than hiring and training in-house employees—thereby helping to enhance both efficiency and resilience. Equally important is how multinationals reconfigure and use internal talent that may be distributed across its different subsidiaries. Companies can create virtual marketplaces for skills to allow subsidiaries to tap into critical skills that might be available elsewhere within the multinational.

For example, consider Unilever's AI-powered FLEX Experiences platform. It was established as an online talent marketplace for Unilever's employees, a way to help them identify new career opportunities and areas where they can upskill via flexible project experience.[9] Employees build a profile of their current skills and specific areas in which they are looking to improve or gain new expertise. The system then uses AI to help individual employees identify a personalized list of open projects across the enterprise, in real time. The initiative ostensibly helps employees build new skills and/or broaden their professional horizons, but it also provides a powerful means to enhance subsidiaries' orchestration capabilities. Specifically, it allows subsidiaries to seek out critical skills and rapidly reconfigure their resources to adapt to new situations. Further, employees contribute only part of their time to such projects, allowing the company to modularize their in-house human resources and optimize their use across the enterprise. As Jeroen Wels, Unilever's executive vice president for human resources, said, "We strongly believe that if people thrive, business will thrive. FLEX Experiences is truly empowering our people to look for opportunities that fit their purpose and follow their interest and energy. It is democratizing careers, liberating, and indeed unleashing talent potential across the globe."[10] Such initiatives can significantly enhance a multinational's ability at regional and local levels to seek out and pull in talent from across the vast enterprise in short order, allowing it to adapt rapidly to an evolving local situation.

Thus such virtualization of skills combined with online internal marketplaces can radically transform how multinationals and their subsidiaries induce greater levels of efficiency and resilience in their global operations—dynamically reconfiguring key skills and talent in cost-effective ways to adapt to evolving situations.

Virtualization of compliance and monitoring. Most multinationals employ extensive and often quite bureaucratic monitoring systems to ensure compliance with local/regional regulations, as well as corporate rules and policies. Often these compliance systems become a critical hurdle to enhance both efficiency and resilience of global operations.

Digitization can help overcome such challenges in global compliance programs. For example, robotic process automation (RPA) can handle exponentially more transactions or checks than humans, and as such it can be leveraged to provide compliance and internal checks and balances for global operations. Similarly, blockchain and related technologies can be used to monitor operations at the local level (e.g., for suppliers) and thereby enhance the transparency at the edges of the multinational's global network. Foxconn, the electronics giant best known as a manufacturer of IPhones, launched a Shanghai start-up called Chained Finance with a Chinese peer-to-peer lender that connects Foxconn and its many small suppliers worldwide (and their suppliers' suppliers) via an Ethereum-based blockchain. The system uses its own token and smart contracts, which are automatically executed to make payments and provide financing in near real time, eliminating a daisy chain of paperwork and, importantly, providing direct monitoring of all transactions to ensure compliance with local regulations and corporate policies.

With massive cross-border operations, multinationals are compelled to work more proactively to implement the necessary digital structure for more effective monitoring, data collection, modeling, analysis, reporting, and other activities mandated by regulatory institutions in various countries and by an organization's own need to improve its corporate ethics and compliance. Further, the cost of global compliance is a major issue for many firms, particularly those lacking the scale to absorb major new initiatives, and leveraging digital technologies (such as blockchain, RPA, and AI) can lower the costs of compliance.

The ongoing digital initiative at Philip Morris International (PMI) is illustrative of how the two models—intelligent hubs and intelligent edges—can coexist. Importantly, it also highlights some of the associated execution challenges.

PMI, a US-listed leading international tobacco company that operates in more than 180 countries, has been on a journey to simultaneously create both digitally enabled intelligent regional hubs for its supply chain operations and intelligent edges for its manufacturing operations in many parts of the world. As Nitin Manoharan, PMI's director of global head enterprise architecture and technology innovation, put it, "Digital technologies such as AI, IoT, and blockchain are enabling us to establish different levels of integration of our operations across the enterprise and also to tie everything together nicely to adapt to both global and local forces."[11]

PMI's approach has been to carefully evaluate how real-time and dynamic the operational information is and what types of localization forces constrain the company's decision-making process and operations. For those units in markets with considerable local forces and time sensitivity, the company pushes the intelligence to the edges and locates analytics and decision-making there. And when such local forces are less dominant and efficiencies can be gained through regional coordination, the company adopts a regional intelligent hub strategy. For example, in some markets, special tax rules apply for finished goods that constrain their movement; in other markets, regulations related to how much material should be sourced from inside a country constrain production decisions. Further, partners in some markets are quite advanced in their use of digital technologies, enabling PMI's access to faster and more accurate information on varied operational needs. The company incorporated such variations across different markets in terms of government regulations, digital infrastructure, and business culture when deciding how to go about implementing its intelligent hub and intelligent edge strategy.

In the global network of production facilities, each production facility needs to be able to respond to changing spatial and temporal dimensions rapidly while allowing the regional and central intelligent hub to focus on the mid- to long-term trends. For instance, at the edge, PMI's production facilities aim to capture data from machine sensors to enable near-real-time decisions on the quality of a batch of products, while the regional and central intelligent hubs analyze data to produce recommendations on improving the recipe in the mid- to long term.

As the company continues its journey along this path, it has also discovered several challenges related to execution. For example, once it implemented sensors in many of its production units, data security threats assumed greater importance. And the company also discovered that the severity of such cybersecurity threats varied from one country to another. Similarly, in different markets, the company found that suppliers and partners have different thresholds with regard to the security of the data that they share in real time with PMI. The application of machine learning that forms the basis for the intelligence posed another set of issues. For example, as Manoharan noted, "While we pushed the intelligence to regional hubs for some of our supply chain operations, it became very difficult to calibrate the prediction models because there's no such thing as a baseline against which you can train it." Also, there are a number of local constraints that can crop up at any time to disrupt the automated decision-making in regional hubs. These and other issues are likely to be present for most companies as they use digital technologies to address the need for both integration and disaggregation.

However, despite all these challenges, a strategy that combines both approaches and makes them contingent on globalization/localization forces can equip a company to achieve the best mix of efficiency and resilience in the long term. PMI's growing investments in ongoing digital initiatives in this area reflect the company's confidence about such future benefits.

Conclusion

We started this chapter by posing questions: How should multinationals navigate the emerging international business landscape that calls for both integration and disaggregation of their subsidiary operations in order to respond to globalization and localization forces at play in different foreign markets? And how does digitization help in addressing this challenge?

Our answer incorporates the careful selection and combination of two alternate models:

1. *Intelligent hub*, in which a few key global hubs of a multinational develop and control critical resources and make them available for subsidiaries in other countries to use

2. *Intelligent edge*, which involves disaggregating global activities to the extent that much of the operational planning and decision-making are conducted at the frontline units or the edges of a multinational's global network, where the subsidiaries reside

A predominant focus on the intelligent hub model, which entails a tight coupling between a company and its subsidiaries, may be appropriate in certain limited contexts. But by combining these two models (intelligent hub/intelligent edge approach), multinationals can institute a loose coupling in their relationships with their subsidiaries. This reflects a key insight from multinationals' recent experiences in adapting to local/regional and global disruptions: building both efficiency and resilience in operations requires sufficient intelligence and orchestration capabilities in both global hubs and in foreign subsidiaries. Further, digital technologies play a critical role in not only enabling such models but also ensuring that reconfiguration of resources and activities carried out are aligned with both local conditions and corporate goals.

In all these discussions, however, we have only briefly discussed a key issue: the organizational capabilities needed to accomplish all this. What capabilities are crucial for multinationals to realize the promise held by new digital technologies and infrastructures for managing global activities? And how should multinationals establish and nurture a digital culture that is appropriate for their purposes? These are questions that we will explore in detail in the last chapter.

Next, we examine a multinational's approach to global innovation and knowledge creation.

6   Connecting with Global Innovation and Knowledge Digitally

Multinational companies serve as a powerful vehicle for the diffusion of innovation across the world—generating innovation in one part of the world and marketing it in another part of the world. Think of Apple and its smartphones or Amazon and its e-commerce services. Traditionally, such a flow of innovation has been from developed economies to developing and emerging economies. In the last decade or so, there has been evidence of a flow of innovation in the reverse direction, too; for example, consider the Chinese company ByteDance and its Tik-Tok social media platform.[1] The rapid waves of digitization that have engulfed companies across industries have radically transformed how they source innovative ideas and assets from international markets, as well as how such innovation assets are reconfigured and recombined to fuel new innovation in other parts of the world.

Indeed, digitization has redefined the global innovation landscape in many different ways. First, digitization of products and offerings have allowed companies to codify and modularize their knowledge and innovative ideas to a much greater extent, enhancing the portability of a company's innovation assets across national borders, as well as allowing for their recombination and reuse in different foreign markets. Companies can mix and match their digital assets, generating innovation in offerings, business models, and operations to suit specific foreign markets—at a much faster pace and at lower cost. For example, Tommy Hilfiger transitioned to an innovative 3D design platform for all its apparel in time for its spring 2022 collection.[2] This allows the company to deploy a fully digital design workflow across all of its global apparel design teams and involves creating, storing, sharing, and reusing digital design assets (including digital fabric, pattern, and color assets) to cater to different global markets. Transforming traditional design and sample production steps into such digital-infused assets and processes enables Tommy Hilfiger to not only accelerate its innovation but also diversify its offerings.

Second, in the past several years, multinational companies have increasingly opened their doors to embrace innovative ideas and resources from outside the organization. Such open innovation approaches rely on global digital infrastructures that connect companies to diverse innovation sources—from customers to supply chain partners to start-ups—spread across the world. For example, companies can use their own digital infrastructure, such as websites, as well as third-party digital platforms to crowdsource ideas from their customers and partners in foreign markets, thereby enhancing the opportunities for innovation. Recent reports indicate that 85 percent of the top global brands and more than 75 percent of the world's high-performing multinational enterprises have used crowdsourcing in the last ten years in one form or another.[3] Indeed, the global digital crowdsourcing market was valued at $9 billion in 2018 and is expected to grow to $154 billion by 2027, indicating the global reach and scope of innovation sourcing practices facilitated by digital platforms.[4]

Third, digitization has started changing the very process of innovation. Uncertainty lies at the core of innovation management, and in recent years the power of modern data analytics has been brought to bear to help managers navigate such innovation uncertainty. Indeed, the emerging field of *innovation analytics* involves the generation and use of data-driven insights and visualizations within innovation processes and seeks to endow business and innovation managers with newfound capabilities to manage uncertainties in product and service innovation.[5] For example, start-ups such as UK-based SoundOut and US-based First Insight and 84.51° have established novel online review platforms that combine the science and rigor of experimentation (involving large numbers of preselected testers or potential customers from across the world) with the power and capabilities of modern AI-based analytics to generate valuable innovation insights for companies across industries.[6] Such digital innovation experimentation forms the frontier of innovation management.

All of these changes indicate the power of digital forces to alter both the nature and the pace of multinational companies' innovation pursuits in global markets.

At the same time, many of the regional/local forces discussed in earlier chapters could hinder companies from realizing the promise and potential of digitization to enhance their innovation success. For example, lack of clarity in IP rights laws and policies in a foreign market could put the brakes on a company's efforts to source innovation from that market. Highly restrictive local data regulations could inhibit the portability and analysis of innovation elsewhere in the world. Similarly, a foreign market's unique local digital infrastructure may prevent companies from deploying digital innovation assets developed in that market elsewhere in the world. Or key aspects of the dominant business culture in a foreign market may prevent a company from establishing trust-based relationships with external partners and pursuing collaborative innovation.

Thus, the confluence of digitization and localization forces poses a broader question for multinational companies. How should companies navigate the emerging global innovation landscape transformed by digitization and localization?

In this chapter, we address this question by focusing on two specific areas of innovation: how companies source innovation assets and other resources from international markets and how companies configure those innovation assets and resources to fuel innovation in products, business models, and operations in different markets. To this end, we consider two key elements of a company's digital global business connectivity in detail.

Elements of Tight and Loose Coupling with Global Digital Innovation

We define two elements of a company's digital global business connectivity with regard to innovation: company-innovation source connectivity and company-innovation asset connectivity.

The first element, *company-innovation source connectivity*, relates to a company's overall approach to seeking and sourcing innovation from different international markets. As we noted earlier, the move from closed to more open innovation accompanied by the global reach offered by digital technologies and platforms allows companies to cast a very wide net for innovation. A broad set of mechanisms are available for this purpose—ranging from electronic R&D marketplaces to internal/external incubators and accelerators.[7] However, these mechanisms vary in terms of the nature and closeness of the relationship between the company and the source of innovation. Some mechanisms rely on more frequent interactions and extensive sharing of information, while others imply a more arm's-length, transactional relationship. Importantly, the use of the different approaches in a foreign market needs to be calibrated based on the intensity of localization forces (regulatory environment, digital infrastructure), allowing for varying degrees of tight and loose coupling.

The second element, *company-innovation asset connectivity*, relates to how a company reconfigures and deploys the digital innovation assets generated in a foreign market along with its other innovation assets and resources. While digital innovation assets are eminently recombinable and reconfigurable, local/regional forces often play a key role in deciding the extent to which such reconfigurations are possible or even desirable. Here, we examine different strategies or approaches multinational companies can adopt with regard to such digital innovation asset reconfiguration, implying different levels of tight and loose coupling.

Let's now consider these two elements in greater detail.

Company-Innovation Source Connectivity and Global Open Innovation

Sourcing Innovation on a Global Scale

A decade or so back, Satish Nambisan and Mohan Sawhney conducted a study comparing and categorizing different innovation-sourcing mechanisms based on the degree of maturity of the innovative ideas

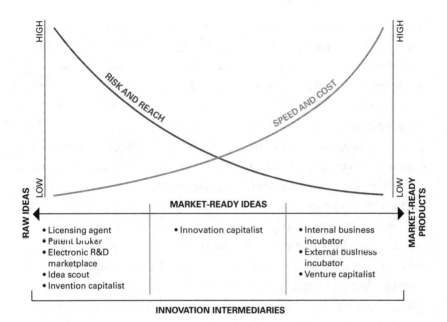

Figure 6.1
Global innovation sourcing mechanisms. Adapted from S. Nambisan and M. Sawhney, "A Buyer's Guide to the Innovation Bazaar," *Harvard Business Review* 85, no. 6 (June 2007): 111.

sourced (see figure 6.1). The focus then was on understanding the trade-offs companies needed to make in choosing among the different sourcing venues, weighing such factors as innovation speed, cost, reach, and risk. For example, idea scouts and online R&D marketplaces (such as InnoCentive) allow for acquiring innovative ideas and solutions in fairly raw form and relatively inexpensively, but those ideas then need to be brought inside the company and developed further. At the other end of the continuum, business incubators and accelerators allow for sourcing market-ready products/services that could be readily commercialized without much additional work; however, such market-ready innovations tend to be rather expensive.

Over the past ten years or so, advances in digital technologies have changed the very nature of many of these trade-offs. For example, digital innovation experimentation platforms that employ data analytics have reduced the cost of testing raw ideas, thereby reducing the associated risks to a considerable extent. Such experimentation also serves as the foundation for a company's iterative innovation processes, allowing for faster and less risky transformation of ideas into finished offerings.

SoundOut, the UK-based start-up we mentioned earlier, helps consumer product companies and retailers test competing new product designs and optimize their new product development decisions. The company has established a global online review platform (that involves a panel of over three million potential customers or testers) to conduct innovation experiments. Experimental data collected through this platform is analyzed using AI-based algorithms that generate valuable insights to guide product development decisions. Such digital innovation experiments can be completed in as short a time frame as twenty-four to forty-eight hours and at very low cost, thereby negating the drawbacks associated with various innovation sourcing mechanisms.

Similarly, Pittsburgh-based First Insight uses structured online "games" to acquire customer inputs on client firms' innovation alternatives. It then employs predictive analytics to generate valuable insights into product design options that are likely to be the most successful, as well as to identify the right retail price (before product release), determine the segments to target, and gauge forecasts for new products. A number of companies, including Marks & Spencer, Kohl's, Hunter Fan Company, and Crate and Barrel, increasingly rely on such digitally enabled, large-scale, rapid experimentation for their innovation decisions.

Digitization may thus render some of the trade-offs moot, but other types of risks and considerations assume significance, particularly in the context of sourcing innovation from international markets. For example, the intensity of regional/local forces shapes the risks associated with information sharing and constrains the nature of a company's relationship with foreign innovation partners. Thus, we now shift our focus from the maturity of the ideas sourced to the extent of knowledge that a company shares with its innovation sources and, more broadly, to the nature of a company's relationship with innovation sources (tightly or loosely coupled). We consider two digitally enabled innovation sourcing strategies—the digital innovation partnership model and the digital innovation hub model—and discuss their relevance in globalized and localized foreign markets.

Tight and Loose Coupling in Company-Innovation Market Connectivity

When companies source innovation from outside the organization or when they pursue collaborative innovation with global partners, the success of such efforts often hinges on two key factors—a clear understanding of what exactly they are looking for and their ability to communicate that information to others.[8] In general, the greater the extent of the shared understanding of the innovation context among the innovation sources or partners, the more valuable their contributions and the greater the innovation success.

Digital technologies can enhance a company's ability to couple tightly with its innovation partners and share innovation-related knowledge with them, but its willingness to do so is shaped by the external environment, including IP protection laws and the prevailing business culture. In more globalized markets, companies may find such factors more predictable and congruent with their expectations and hence more favorable to establishing tightly coupled partner relationships—more frequent interactions and a greater extent of information sharing. This enables them to identify common areas of interest and have a more open exchange of ideas. We refer to this as the *digital partnership model*, underlining both the closeness of the relationships with foreign innovation sources and the critical role of digital technologies in enabling those relationships (see table 6.1).

The digital partnership model involves pursuing collaborative innovation projects with a few selected foreign partners in a highly focused problem area. While the broader structure of such innovation partnership agreements has remained the same over the years, the nature and extent of the digital coupling possible between innovation partners has radically changed in the last several years, transforming the very process of innovation. For example, digitization or virtualization of innovation

Table 6.1
Strategies for company-innovation source connectivity

| Strategy | Intensity of localization forces | | | Nature of coupling |
	Government regulations and policies	Digital infrastructure	Business culture	
Digital partnership	Low	Low to moderate	Low	Tight coupling
Digital hub	Moderate to high	High	Moderate to high	Loose coupling

processes has allowed multinationals to establish highly secure virtual spaces for foreign partners to share and, using AI and other methods, rapidly analyze different types of data (including live data streams from customer-facing units) that inform ideation; conduct immersive virtual reality (VR) hackathons to develop product concepts; simulate and test virtual prototypes that inform critical design and scaling issues; and, more broadly, enhance the overall transparency of partner innovation activities and contributions.

For instance, a large medical device multinational was designing a new product that had both hardware and software components.[9] While the company was making the hardware platform, the software and associated components were the responsibility of three foreign partners, two in EU countries and one in India. A key challenge in such projects is that software development has to wait until at least the functional prototypes of the hardware platform are developed, potentially delaying the whole project. However, in this case, the manufacturer overcame that by developing and sharing a digital twin of the hardware platform with its foreign partners. On a secure virtual space, the company and its foreign partners jointly conducted simulations on the digital twin that informed both hardware and software design and allowed those to proceed in parallel. The tight digital coupling that the medical devices company established with its three foreign partners allowed it to accelerate the project but also, importantly, enhanced its visibility into its partners' product development activities. At the same time, such data sharing and digitally enabled interactions, which underlie a digital partnership, require a close alignment between the multinational and its foreign partners in terms of business norms and practices, digital infrastructure, and regional data policies and regulations. In this particular case, the conditions in the three foreign partners' countries were deemed favorable for the multinational to proceed with establishing digital tight coupling. On the other hand, if there are strong localization forces in any of the partner countries, the promise held by advanced digital technologies for such tight coupling may become moot.

Consider another case, that of Bayer subsidiary Climate, which leads the digital agriculture market with its FieldView platform. It illustrates how such a digital partnership model translates into the platform context. To promote innovation on its FieldView platform, in the last couple of years, the company has been pursuing collaborations with partners in some globalized markets, including Canada, Israel, and the EU. For example, it has forged partnerships with several start-ups in related market spaces, including Agribotix (drone-based agricultural intelligence company), SoilOptix (a soil mapping company), and Ceres Imaging (an aerial imagery company). The company has also developed close partnership with major equipment companies such as John Deere and AGCO. All of these partnerships involve a carefully designed vetting process, considerable sharing of data and other digital platform-specific assets (including closed API keys), and extensive one-on-one interactions on varied innovation issues. The tight coupling between the company and its foreign partners has been predicated not only on shared innovation goals, but also on the adherence in those countries to global standards related to trade, infrastructure, and business practices.

Another approach to digital partnership has been to locate a multinational's R&D/innovation centers in different parts of the world and to tie them together digitally to ensure coherent innovation efforts. For example, DuPont has built a connected network of innovation centers across the world, including sites in Brazil, Switzerland, Russia,

China, India, and Taiwan. The digital connectivity between the centers allows for rapid sharing of data and other digital innovation assets across national borders (using safe and secure digital infrastructures), enabling DuPont to pursue innovation projects that leverage talent and competencies present in multiple countries. Many other US multinationals—including Cisco, Caterpillar, Goldman Sachs, Google, and Oracle—have located parts of their R&D efforts in different parts of Asia to tap into the enormous talent available there, despite challenges related to IP rights management and other factors in some countries.[10] Many of these R&D centers also partner with local start-ups in those foreign markets to pursue innovative technologies—in effect, adopting the partnership strategy.

However, recent shifts in the nature and intensity of localization forces in China—particularly, worsening US-China trade disputes, illustrated best by the US ban on business with Huawei and the tit-for-tat move by China to ban business with Qualcomm—have triggered a rethink by several US multinationals on their global R&D sourcing and partnership strategies. For example, some multinationals, like Oracle, have started shifting their R&D centers partly or fully away from China, indicating how the digital partnership model is predicated on having stable and favorable business environments, including trade policies, shared business culture, and well-established IP laws and policies. When there is a widening gap between a company's expectations about knowledge sharing and the prevailing trade, IP policies, and related factors in a foreign market, the digital innovation hub model assumes greater relevance.

Many multinational companies across industries, including BT Group (formerly British Telecom), Siemens, McDonald's, Johnson Controls, and Procter & Gamble, have established incubators, accelerators, crowdsourcing platforms, and other open innovation structures in different parts of the world to channel innovative technologies and ideas in from the outside. *Digital innovation hubs* can be considered an evolution of such corporate incubators and accelerators in that they provide a common space (virtual or physical hub) for a multinational and a wide range of partners (typically, start-ups) to come together and explore one another's innovation assets and goals and pursue joint development efforts. However, unlike traditional incubators/accelerators, digital innovation hubs recognize that data and digital connectivity are key for success in most innovation initiatives; as such, they focus on providing the digital backbone that enables not only different types of partner engagement but also different types of collaborative innovation processes.

For example, Intel recently set up an accelerator in Israel called Ignite to tap into that country's innovation sources. In early 2020, Ignite transformed itself into a virtual accelerator, whereby many of the interactions and knowledge exchanges between Intel and its partners occurred via digital platforms. The Unilever Foundry provides yet another illustration of a digital innovation hub. The initiative's aim is to enable Unilever to engage with external partners in order to develop and scale technology-based solutions tailored to specific business challenges, particularly in connecting with the company's customers the world over. For instance, in Singapore, the Unilever Foundry not only acts as a coworking hub for the company and its partners but also facilitates partner interactions and data sharing through a wide range of digital tools and platforms. Also, by locating the innovation hub within the company's regional headquarters, the company provides start-ups with unrivalled access to Unilever brands and other business aspects that are critical for experimenting with different solutions.

The nature of such connectivity in the digital innovation hub can be calibrated based on the intensity of localization forces in a foreign market. UK-based pharmaceutical company AstraZeneca's BioVentureHub, located in Sweden, is a case in point. BioVentureHub constitutes an attempt to pursue open innovation that is based on closeness but with appropriate regulatory control and IP orientation.[11] Notably, a digital backbone provides application-level data connectivity across the different companies or BioVentureHub members; member companies (data owners) can separately decide what data or information they want to share and on what terms.[12]

The unique characteristic of digital innovation hubs is how digitization enables careful design of partner relationships, even varying across different partners within a hub. As the Unilever Foundry and other such innovation initiatives indicate, the extent of sharing of digital assets in innovation hubs can be specified at the level of a region or market or even at the level of individual partners. Digital technologies can thus anchor and support a multinational's engagement with different innovation partners, but the company still has to continually calibrate, experiment with, and adapt the nature of its innovation engagement with changing localization forces. And to that extent, as Tzahi Weisfeld, Ignite's general manager, noted, "We are heading towards a new world."[13] This world is one in which digital technologies become the primary tool to balance the promise of collaborative innovation with risks due to localization forces.

To summarize our discussion so far, the digital partnership model implies tight coupling between a company and its innovation sources. It relies on close, interaction-heavy relationships and considerable sharing of information, both formally and informally. It allows for a greater level of responsiveness: companies can adapt the nature and extent of their relationships with foreign partners (and the innovation sourced from them) based on their changing corporate-level innovation needs. However, the considerable extent of effort that has to go into building such interaction-heavy relationships also limits the number of foreign partners, potentially lowering the distinctiveness of the innovations sourced. Digital innovation hubs, on the other hand, imply loose coupling between a company and its foreign market innovation sources. It allows companies to reach far and wide and connect with relevant partners in a foreign market, thereby enhancing the distinctiveness of the innovative ideas and solutions obtained. At the same time, the underlying digital frameworks of the innovation hubs allow multinationals to adapt the nature and extent of partner engagement to fit both the local conditions and the corporate goals and priorities, thereby retaining some level of responsiveness.

Company-Innovation Asset Connectivity

Digital Assets and Recombinant Innovation

As a company accumulates more and more digital assets (whether as part of its offerings or operational processes), opportunities for recombining those assets in different ways to generate new innovation also increase. Indeed, an important consequence of the digitization of products and processes is the increased ability of companies to reconfigure existing ideas in new ways to make new ideas—a process called *recombinant innovation*. Such cross-pollination and recombination of digital assets, along with new business logic, can lead to novel value creation opportunities in different parts of the world.

A case in point is the smart home market, which is expected to grow from about $85 billion in 2020 to about $140 billion in 2023.[14] As the number of digital components in home appliances and devices increased over the last few years, so did the opportunity to recombine these different digital assets and the data they produce in different ways to create new value for customers. Such home-based digital assets are present in simple devices such as video doorbells, outdoor cameras, smart locks, and smart speakers, as well as in more complex home appliances such as heating, ventilation, air conditioning, and refrigeration systems. When combined with new digital technologies and platforms such as IoT, 5G, blockchain, and AI, these diverse digital assets allow companies to offer a potpourri of solutions to fit different markets.

Digital assets include a diverse range of resources, including digital product components, digital processes (virtual manufacturing and logistics operations), data (generated from operations and market transactions), and digital content (digital design documents and digital brand and marketing materials). The number of digital asset types and classifications has been increasing exponentially with the infusion of digital technologies into all aspects of business. The sheer range and amount of such digital assets accumulating day by day within a company imply the promise and potential of recombinant innovation unleashed by digitization.

Digital assets have monetary value that can be unlocked through reconfiguration and reuse in different contexts. Thus digital assets imply the potential to generate more value through continued sharing and reuse. At the same time, to realize such value, companies will need to ensure two key conditions.

First, digital assets have to be organized in a form that makes them easily discoverable and accessible across the organization. Digital asset management tools have gained much prominence in the last few years to address this need. A recent industry report ranked digital asset management as a top-three digital priority for large organizations.[15] The global digital asset management market is anticipated to grow at about 16.5 percent to reach $8.5 billion by 2025.[16] Cloud-based digital asset management solutions allow companies to not only store digital assets (along with their metadata and "right to use" information) but also find, share, adapt, and deploy those assets with speed and agility. Thus digital asset management tools increasingly form a cornerstone of a company's collaborative innovation efforts by serving as the connective tissue across an organization in the reconfiguration of digital assets.

Second, it is not enough to simply find and generate new combinations of digital assets; companies also need to be able to judiciously select from among the different possibilities or combinations. As economist Martin Weitzman noted way back in 1998, the limits to growth from recombinant innovation "lie not so much in our ability to generate new ideas as in our ability to process an abundance of potentially new ideas into usable form."[17] And this is where AI technologies become valuable. For example, machine learning techniques can not only enhance the visibility into a company's digital asset repositories but also use metadata (the contextual data about digital assets) to analyze and identify possible constraints in their recombination and use in different foreign markets. AI could also be used to decipher patterns among digital assets and connect them with specific market needs and contexts. In other words, AI techniques could potentially inform companies of the relative appeal of the different value paths derived by combining or connecting different digital assets.

For a multinational enterprise, digital assets represent firm-specific assets that could be reconfigured and deployed in foreign markets. Importantly, many such digital assets may also be created and reside locally in a foreign market and not necessarily in its home country. Thus even when a company possesses the ability to find these digital assets and rapidly adapt them for new contexts, local and regional forces may play a critical moderating role, sometimes augmenting and other times diminishing the ability to redeploy digital assets. For example, the right to use a digital asset (even one owned by a company) may be restricted by national borders or other local laws and regulations. Better understanding of these local/regional forces may allow companies to fashion appropriate strategies that involve tight or loose coupling with their digital assets in different foreign markets, finding ways to maximize the value that could be generated from them. Here we examine two broad strategies in this regard and illustrate them with some examples.

Tight and Loose Coupling in Company-Innovation Asset Connectivity

The ease with which value can be unlocked from a digital asset is dependent on how quickly and inexpensively a company can move the asset from one location (context) to another and how effectively it can be combined with other assets in the new context. As noted earlier, to a great extent, digital asset management tools can automate and speed up the selection and distribution of digital assets within a company. But their easy recombination will depend on how well the asset is aligned with the data and digital infrastructure and usage policies in the local context.

In highly globalized foreign markets, the data and digital infrastructures, data usage, and IP policies are likely to adhere closely to a commonly accepted set of global standards and expectations. This would allow multinational enterprises to maintain a common portfolio of digital assets wedded to such standards and to extend the same easily to foreign markets. Such a *global digital asset reconfiguration approach*

Table 6.2
Strategies for company-innovation asset connectivity

Strategy	Intensity of localization			Nature of coupling
	Government regulations and policies	Digital infrastructure	Business culture	
Global asset reconfiguration	Low	Low	Low	Tight coupling
Regional asset reconfiguration	Moderate to high	Moderate to high	Moderate to high	Loose coupling

(see table 6.2) entails a common set of processes and standards to create and manage all digital assets—whether created in a foreign market or imported there from elsewhere—thereby accelerating asset recombination and generating greater value from individual digital assets. On the other hand, in the presence of more localized digital infrastructures, data use policies, and other regulations in a foreign market, companies may need to develop and maintain a digital asset portfolio that is more loosely coupled with its other corporate digital assets. We refer to this as the *regional digital asset reconfiguration approach*. Such a "walled" approach reflects the need for greater adherence to local constraints and rules, as well as a greater focus on regional/local digital asset reuse than on global reuse.

Take the case of Johnson Controls, the $32 billion multinational conglomerate that dominates the building technologies market.[18] The company currently offers a whole range of building technologies—from heating, ventilation, and air conditioning systems to fire, security, and building management systems. For much of its history, the company was a leader in innovating and manufacturing various electromechanical devices for enhancing building efficiency and comfort, but by the 1990s and the 2000s, the company's fortunes were in decline as low-cost competitors elsewhere in the world became more dominant. Thus, starting in the early 2010s, the company returned to its roots in automation and control and started reinventing itself digitally. Most of the offerings related to the company's main four units—fire, security,

HVAC, and controls—were digitized, transforming the very ways in which the company innovates.

In response to growing demand for intelligent interconnected building management systems, the company developed a sophisticated, cloud-based digital solution that fully leverages the capabilities of IoT, sensor-based real-time data collection, edge computing, cloud-based analytics, AI, and machine learning—in effect, offering an entire smart building ecosystem for its clients. The real-time data collected and analyzed inform facility managers of energy usage, security breaches, building equipment performance, space optimization, and a host of other performance factors.

In becoming such a pure-play intelligent building management company, the broader approach for Johnson Controls has been to develop and maintain a rapidly growing portfolio of versatile digital assets—all founded on new and powerful technologies—that can be used in different combinations to cater to different markets. The company also allows for creating common, structured data depositories on which innovative applications can be built at scale (by mixing and matching the digital assets) to fit specific customer needs. To this end, Johnson Controls launched its open digital platform, OpenBlue, which brings together all its digital assets and allows for combining data from both inside and outside buildings. As the company's CEO, George Oliver, noted, OpenBlue "reflects how we think buildings are evolving from inflexible assets to dynamic resources."[19]

The company's progress in such a digital innovation initiative illustrates both global asset reconfiguration and regional asset reconfiguration approaches and the importance it places on localization forces in different international markets. As Mike Ellis, the company's chief digital officer and chief customer officer, noted, in driving digital innovation, Johnson Controls takes advantage of its global footprint efficiently and with great technologies—but at the same time, it tailors its approach to the regions that it operates in.[20] The company uses a common set of digital technologies and standards across its different units, allowing for the digital assets to be easily moved across borders and combined with other digital assets, but it also takes into consideration regional factors that are likely to shape the risks and benefits of use and reuse of those digital assets.

For example, the company started its digitization initiative in early 2010s with the *China first* theme promoted by then CEO Alex Molinaroli, acknowledging the blue-sky opportunity China offered for digital innovation experimentation and development. While the company pursued several promising projects that involved the application of AI and machine learning, it was clear from the start that much of the digital asset development effort would be tightly embedded in the local digital/data infrastructure and market context, emphasizing digital asset reuse and recombinations within the region rather than globally—in effect, following a regional asset reconfiguration approach. For instance, a key focus in China has been on building smart hospitals, which has required the company to not only partner with local healthcare organizations but also leverage data that are founded on localized digital infrastructures, thereby limiting their portability and relevance for the global market. Similarly, another early project involved enhancing the efficiency of sales and marketing operations in China by developing extensive digital marketing repositories and employing AI to guide their use in different contexts. Again, though the ideas behind the digital innovation initiative had broader relevance, the company soon realized that the digital assets that were developed could not be easily ported and reused outside the country. Indeed, as one senior executive noted, the digital innovation initiatives launched in China did not necessarily contribute to the company's global asset portfolio; however, the company did derive some important lessons on digital innovation and digital asset management, which were then utilized when it started similar initiatives in Belgium, starting with business process optimization through digital technologies.

On the other hand, Johnson Controls' recently announced partnership with the Singapore Economic Development Board to establish an innovation lab in Singapore represents the global asset reconfiguration approach. The initiative will leverage local research organizations and other technology partners in Singapore, but the key focus will be on

developing digital assets—especially those that blend building, spatial, and behavioral data with IoT, edge computing, AI, and machine
learning—that can contribute to the company's digital solutions for
the Asia-Pacific and global markets. Indeed, the initiative is largely
premised on Singapore's attractiveness as a location for companies to
develop and commercialize new digital solutions for the global market. Recall the DHL Global Connectedness Index that we mentioned
in chapter 2. Singapore is ranked number 2 in the index, indicating its
highly globalized business environment.

The focus on pursuing digital innovation with a regional/local or
global scope in terms of digital asset reconfiguration is largely shaped
by data policies and regulations in a foreign market. As in the case of
Johnson Controls, many multinationals realize this up front, based on
a careful evaluation of the localization forces. For example, Unilever
recently established an innovation hub—called an AI hub—in Shanghai that is exclusively focused on developing innovation assets "in
China and for China," indicating the company's regional asset reconfiguration approach. There is one good reason for that. Although the
AI hub will employ high-performance computers and a bevy of other
digital tools equipped with modeling and AI/data analytics capabilities
to virtually design, develop, and test new product concepts, it will also
incorporate real-time local market and consumer data in the innovation
process. For example, livestreaming has become a huge sensation in
e-commerce in China, and the AI hub will tap into and use information
from these streams to capture and predict trends and guide the innovation efforts. At the same time, given the peculiarity of the e-commerce
data streams and the foundational digital infrastructure in China, the
machine learning algorithms and other digital assets will also be localized, limiting their reuse and recombination to the regional context.
However, as Unilever senior executive Zaved Akhtar noted, the AI hub
in China does provide "a broader template that can be replicated in
other parts of the world," in ways that can contribute to the company's
global innovation assets.[21] In other words, depending on the international market context—whether globalized or localized—the same

innovation structure could represent different approaches to innovation asset reconfiguration and value creation.

Conclusion

We began this chapter with a question: How should multinational companies navigate the global innovation landscape that is being radically transformed by both digitization and localization forces?

Our answer here incorporates two sets of prototypical strategies:

1. *Digital partnership* and *digital hub* strategies, which relate to a multinational's relationship with global innovation sources (partners) in terms of the closeness and intensity of interactions and the nature and extent of sharing of innovation assets

2. *Global asset reconfiguration* and *regional asset reconfiguration* strategies, which relate to how a multinational manages its digital asset portfolio and the scope of asset reuse and recombination it promotes

Importantly, the focus on innovation sourcing and innovation usage reflected in these strategies are two sides of the same coin. Innovation assets sourced from one foreign market may find less value if local conditions limit their portability and reconfiguration in another market. For example, a company may pursue an innovation by sourcing a digital innovation asset from a partner in a foreign market and then combining that with its own digital asset. But local policies may limit the portability of the partner's asset, thereby raising questions about the company's investments in the innovation initiative. Further, such local constraints are often dynamic; policies related to IP rights, data storage, and data privacy may all be continuously evolving. A critical challenge for companies then is to ensure alignment between innovation sourcing strategies and innovation asset reconfiguration strategies across different markets and businesses so as to maximize the value from their digital assets.

Next, we'll discuss internationalizing business models in the digital age.

7 Internationalizing Business Models Digitally

A viable global business model has strong implications for international businesses due to creating a unique and sustained competitive position. A successful business model, whether adopted nationally, regionally, or globally, tends to have a certain degree of embeddedness within the multinational—that is, the extent to which it is enabled (or constrained) by a set of unique processes or capabilities possessed by the company. Think of Netflix's superior data analysis capabilities or Etsy's unique relationship with creatives. Although business models can be imitated, such embeddedness affords business model pioneers a competitive advantage for a certain period of time. Further, a global business model template can provide an overall architecture to rapidly bring together the various components of the multinational's internal system—its strategy, structure, and resources—in a foreign market. It allows companies to specialize and move more quickly to seize new growth opportunities as they emerge in different parts of the world and make better use of global open resources that align well with the firms' strengths. For example, much of Louis Vuitton's success has come from using the same business model as it expanded globally: selling its products through stand-alone boutiques in high-end department stores in every country it entered.

But many multinational companies fail when replicating their home-grown business models in other countries. Consider a few well-known examples of US companies failing to port their business models successfully to China. Home Depot realized that its DIY business model doesn't translate well in China. Many Chinese people buy homes for investment and speculation, not to improve them. Further, cheap labor prompts most people to simply hire a handyman. China is a do-it-for-me market, not a do-it-yourself one. Similarly, eBay's online auction model failed in China largely because it neglected to realize the importance of building social connections between buyers and sellers in a country where the rule of law is weak but social ties and interpersonal trust are essential.

All things being equal, a multinational's business model is more likely to be transferable to and applicable in other national settings when the firm serves global customers (demands are not highly differentiated across nations). However, institutional, regulatory, legal, sociocultural, and infrastructural conditions may also come into play in affecting the transferability of a business model to different countries; formal institutional conditions may determine whether certain business models or certain activities of the business model are permitted. Informal institutional conditions also may affect transferability because the consumer value proposition is susceptible to the influence of consumption culture and norms prevalent in the target market. Indeed, the earlier examples of Home Depot and eBay illustrate how differences in consumer culture (DIY orientation) and business culture (source of trust) could derail a company's plan to deploy its global business model.

Infrastructural conditions also matter because fully executing a business model will inevitably rely on a host country's supporting industries, such as logistics and digital infrastructure, to create and deliver the consumer value proposition to target customers. Amazon, for example, closed its domestic marketplace in China in July 2019, ending a tough fifteen-year battle against Alibaba and JD.com in the world's most populous country. Like Amazon, Alibaba and JD.com use a business-to-consumer (B2C) model, but they are more adaptive to and better serve the needs of both small businesses (by offering loans and commercial credit) and consumers (by bundling with Alipay or WeChat Pay). In contrast to Amazon, Walmart continually performs well in China largely due to its business model success. Walmart's overseas location strategy for its brick-and-mortar presence (a central downtown area that mass consumers can access via subways), along with strong networks with local ecosystem partners (including JD.com), has contributed to its success as China's supersized store chain.

Such disparities in the success of internationalizing business models can be explained not only by how well a multinational has adapted its global business model template to fit a foreign market (in terms of regulatory conditions, infrastructure, and culture) but also by how effectively it has used digital technologies in such an internationalizing process. In other words, it is not enough to merely recognize the need to adapt a business model to a new market context. It is equally important to realize how such adaptation can be practiced effectively with the help of digital technologies. In this chapter, we provide a sharper focus on how multinationals can internationalize their business models in the contemporary, highly digitized global business landscape.

Digital Global Business Connectivity and Business Model Internationalization

How Digitization Alters the Internationalization Process

Digital technologies have the potential to change the very process of internationalization. While some of these issues have been highlighted in earlier chapters, it is perhaps worth repeating them in the context of business models.

First, *distance matters less* when digitization drives business model internationalization. Digitization helps multinationals to provide customer value propositions that solve distance-related problems effectively—for example, the problem of getting products to a customer via a global e-commerce platform. Digital connectivity also loosens "liabilities of foreignness" by giving firms new, less time-bound ways of acquiring knowledge and learning about doing business abroad. Firms today can learn enormously about the host country from widely available information resources without a physical presence or learn about establishing local legitimacy via radical acquisitions. More broadly, geographical distance concerns are alleviated to a great extent when business functions and processes can be virtualized.

Second, digitization has made foreign investment commitments *less incremental*. The *conventional view* is that multinationals can only acquire site-specific knowledge or make resource and market commitments through a gradual process.[1] Yet digital connectivity has created ample opportunities for multinationals to leapfrog—a notion labeled as the *springboard view*.[2] At the core of this view lies the argument that multinationals recursively use international expansion as a springboard, facilitated in large part by global digital business connectivity, to more easily and quickly access both upstream and downstream resources of other firms, allowing them to compete more effectively against global rivals at home and abroad and to reduce their vulnerability to institutional and market constraints at home.

Third, with digitization, *path dependence matters less*. Business model internationalization was once reserved for large, long-established companies (often from the Western economies). But digitization has reduced the minimum scale and scope needed to go global, enabling small businesses and new ventures to internationalize their business models rapidly and negating the path-dependence benefits of larger multinationals. All of this has led to new global players (digital disrupters and emerging market multinationals) that are generally lean, agile, aggressive, and cost advantageous. A case in point is South Korea's GP Club, founded by Kim Jung-Woong. In little more than two years, the company has pushed aside giant global and local competitors to create a $1.3 billion company from skin care masks (under the JMsolution brand) that Chinese consumers cannot stop buying. Its quick success lies in one form of digital global business connectivity in China: *daigou* (in Mandarin), or "to buy on behalf of," the practice of purchasing sought-after goods overseas to resell back home digitally, often through WeChat—which had about 1.2 billion active monthly users as of 2020.

Fourth, with digitization, cross-border *mergers and acquisitions have gained prevalence* as a tool for business model internationalization. Foreign direct investments made by multinationals are often aimed at lowering labor and production costs through physical moves or production relocation and through geographical expansion by establishing wholly owned or joint venture facilities. But digitization has weakened the impetus for such physical moves or relocation, making coproduction and codevelopment overseas more viable. On the other hand, cross-border mergers and acquisitions have become a plausible and often quicker solution for expanding international footholds and transferring successful business models from established markets to new markets. This is increasingly true for multinationals from emerging economies too. For example, Natura, a Brazil-based multinational cosmetics and personal care manufacturer, has pursued such a mergers and acquisitions approach to internationalize rapidly. It acquired UK-based the Body Shop (for $1.2 billion) in 2017, Australia's Aesop (for $68 million) in 2014, and Avon of the United States (for $2 billion) in 2019. In all these acquisitions and their subsequent operations, one thing is common: Natura's core business model, focused on delivering contextually customized customer experiences with the use of digital technologies. Ninety-nine percent of its product order transactions are performed digitally, and the company employs a dedicated digital platform (which incorporates customer relationship management [CRM] and advanced data analytics) to conduct a robust analysis of all customer touchpoints and to connect with its thousands of beauty consultants.

How Digitization Shapes a Global Business Model

A *business model* depicts how a firm creates and captures value, including a unique activity and resource structure and an innovative customer value proposition, plus a scheme for capturing and allocating economic value.[3] On the one hand, business models for international businesses should be globally scalable and to some degree stable and transferable across borders. On the other hand, these models must be flexible and dynamic if they are to succeed in many varied and rapidly changing international settings. This suggests the importance of multidexterity in the design of global business models—enveloping the globally consistent umbrella of the model and each local adaptation—and implies how each of the dimensions (and associated elements) of digital global business connectivity described in chapters 3–6 relate to business model internationalization.

Global digital platforms (such as e-commerce marketplaces) allow companies to instantly create direct channels to connect with foreign markets in ways that were all but impossible only a decade or so ago, thereby refashioning one key element of their business model—the value delivery mechanism—to suit the local context. Similarly, social media and other digital channels help companies establish direct linkages between their brands and global customers, enabling companies to reinterpret their value proposition in ways that fit with the consumer culture in different markets. Yet a key challenge for multinationals using such digital services relates to achieving some level of global consistency across channels and devices and at the same time adapting to different foreign market idiosyncrasies. For example, L'Oréal, the world's leading beauty company, uses a single platform (Demandware) for digital consumer engagement management across all channels, including web, mobile, store, and social, for more than twenty-five distinct brands. Such a single digital platform policy has allowed the company to scale easily to support hundreds of worldwide e-commerce sites and other digital touch points. This reach enables L'Oréal to ensure consistent global branding across channels and devices while having the ability to establish distinct experiences for each unique brand and geography.

Digital global business connectivity also fosters entirely new forms of collaboration and dependencies, pushing international businesses to frame their business models in terms of local/regional networks (or business ecosystems) more than ever before. While such network structures help accelerate business model internationalization, they also have two important consequences for multinationals. First, they expose multinationals to new partners with varied business models and cost bases, partners that could potentially become the rivals of tomorrow. This intermingling of different business models can trigger a multinational's own business model innovation efforts. Second, as the multinational's business model anchors the ecosystem, the level of competition shifts from firms to ecosystems, forcing companies to adopt a broader ecosystem perspective in designing business models.

Digital global business connectivity also allows companies to connect with global open resources in foreign markets. This availability has changed many firms' global business models, allowing them to emphasize distinctive activities or processes by which they maintain competitive advantages while taking advantage of global open resources via cross-licensing, alliances, and acquisitions. The market landscape for acquiring resources is now quite different from a decade or more ago in terms of the presence and availability of various intermediary resources or inputs, including professional industrial design, applied technologies, assembled key components, distribution specialists, total logistics solution providers, and advertising and promotion specialists, among others.

Finally, the modularity and standards that underlie digital infrastructures and platforms have allowed for greater extent of cross-sharing key resources—from components and supply bases to distribution channels—among multinationals within an industry, as well as across different industries. Digital global business connectivity also enables transferring operational ownership of one or more business processes to foreign country entities that conduct or manage the services according to predefined metrics. All of these have allowed for multinationals to unpack their business models in different ways (mixing and matching different elements) to suit different regional and market contexts without losing their ability to monitor and coordinate activities spread across different parts of the world.

Innovating Global Business Models for the Digital Age

Digital technology capabilities and affordances combined with the localization imperatives presented by international market contexts propel many multinational companies to innovate on their global business models. There are several avenues for business model innovation; here we highlight a few that are innately tied to digital platforms and digital infrastructures.

Partnerships with local/regional platforms play an essential role in enabling multinationals to rapidly rethink their focal value proposition to fit different foreign markets. Recall Bayer's digital agricultural platform that we discussed in chapter 4. As we noted, the value proposition it offers to farmers in the EU and in North and South America are not appropriate for markets such as India, where farmers have less landholding and use less powerful and versatile digital devices. As such, the company has used partnerships with local platforms as the central strategy to redefine its business model and localize the value proposition. For example, Bayer Crop Science has partnered with ITC, an Indian multinational conglomerate, to use its digital agriplatform e-Choupal 4.0 (which serves as a local marketplace for farmers and also provides a host of on-demand advisory services) as an alternate channel to connect with Indian farmers.[4] This allows Bayer to innovate on value delivery and extend the reach of its crop advisory services in the Indian market. More importantly, it enables Bayer to present its value offerings in conjunction with more localized value offerings, thereby reinterpreting its value proposition in localized terms.

Such partnerships that redefine a value proposition to cater to local markets could also involve multiple global companies coming together to pool their capabilities in unique ways. For instance, French telecommunication giant Orange S.A. and American software company Red Hat (which is now part of IBM) work together to create localized value propositions for clients in Africa and the Middle East. Orange launched a digital center in Tunisia to help provide support for start-up companies through digital transformation and local innovation. Orange and Red Hat codeveloped a horizontal cloud platform in this region. Orange focuses on network transformation through digitization, while Red Hat offers a multivendor, multiapplication network that makes use of everything cloud computing can offer. Similarly, in Egypt, Red Hat provides a software-defined distributed architecture that allows Orange

Egypt to enact services like cybersecurity and malware protection in a way that is tailored to fit its local customers.

Another approach to business model innovation relates to positioning a global digital (data) platform on top of a local (physical) ecosystem to create value. A good illustration of this is given by the medical device and pharma industries. For example, with the US Food and Drug Administration (FDA) relaxing restrictions on where human trials of new drugs and medical devices must be conducted, many multinationals have started hosting some of their product trials in countries such as India and Brazil to minimize costs. The patients who undergo the trial, their doctors and hospitals, and the associated medical services all are part of the local health ecosystem, but the data collected from such trials are channeled through the multinational's own global digital platform. This helps to not only reduce the cost of such trials but also ensure high levels of accuracy and reliability. The challenge is then to ensure appropriate integration of the global digital platform with the local physical ecosystem, and this in turn requires sufficiently trained local talent, appropriate digitized monitoring and reporting systems, and alignment with the local digital infrastructure. The examples from the health sector relate to product development, but the broader insights here relate to the opportunities that exist for multinationals to innovate in their business models by combining their global digital platforms with local/ regional business ecosystems to create localized value offerings. The challenge then is to come up with novel mechanisms—processual, infrastructural, and cultural elements—that connect them effectively to create and deliver value.

The scope of digitized business models can also be easily modified or extended to serve adjacent (or even unrelated) markets and imply yet another avenue for business model innovation in foreign markets. Specifically, a multinational may port its offerings to a foreign market with more or less the same value proposition that it offered in its home country, but it may then discover a new opportunity in that foreign market that could be addressed with the same value creation/delivery platform, an opportunity that did not exist in its home country. For example, much of Chinese drone manufacturer DJI's international expansion success can be attributed to its ability to innovate in its primary business model and value proposition to cater to newer adjacent markets in different foreign markets. Such opportunities may also exist in other foreign markets, indicating the broader promise of such business model innovation.

Conclusion

A business model is configurational and describes, as a system, how the different pieces of a business fit together, with a focus on the two most fundamental elements of the business: the customer (via unique value propositions) and profit (via unique revenue generation). Both of these elements are dependent on the idiosyncrasies of a foreign market and denote the need to localize business models. Indeed, the very process of internationalizing business models to fit different foreign markets can trigger novel ways of creating, delivering, and appropriating value—that is, business model innovations.

Our discussion shows how the digitized nature of business models makes such innovations feasible and scalable, and it illustrates two key takeaways:

1. *Partnerships with local and regional digital platforms in different foreign markets* can enable multinationals to reinterpret their focal value propositions in highly localized terms, thus enhancing their market fit.

2. *Multinationals can innovate on their business models* by (a) combining their global digital platforms with local/regional business (physical) ecosystems to create localized value offerings and/or (b) adapting the scope of their digitized business models to serve adjacent (unrelated) markets in different regions.

At the same time, executing on such business model innovations is not without hurdles and challenges. Often, this process might entail fundamental changes that affect many parts of the multinational enterprise, especially in terms of how the multinational connects with its local subsidiaries in the foreign markets where the innovation happens. No matter how much autonomy is delegated to such strategic business units or frontline subsidiaries, executing or innovating a business model requires global planning, cross-border coordination, headquarter control, top management support, and interunit sharing, all of which can create unexpected obstacles. Although that discussion is beyond the scope of this book, we will look at some of the organizational capabilities needed to overcome such obstacles later in chapter 10.

Next, we consider how digitization has transformed global entrepreneurship.

8 Global Entrepreneurship in the Digital Age

Loulou Khazen Baz, originally from Lebanon, started her entrepreneurial venture Nabbesh—the Arab world's first online employment marketplace—in Dubai in 2012. (*Nabbesh* means *search* in Arabic.) Although Khazen Baz had some prior corporate experience, there were three other main factors that helped her pursue her entrepreneurial initiative. First, the company targeted the Middle Eastern and North African (MENA) region—a region that was experiencing relatively high unemployment and at the same time had many people seeking independence and choice in their work, leading them to the freelance route. Second, Dubai's rapidly growing entrepreneurial ecosystem offered Khazen Baz access to the right set of partners, supporters, and advisors. Third, and more importantly, the digital revolution had reached the MENA region by then, setting the stage for launching a digital platform that could connect local businesses with hundreds or thousands of freelancers. Over the past ten years or so, Nabbesh grew significantly to become the Arab world's largest freelance marketplace, with more than one hundred thousand freelancers and catering to a wide range of national and international companies, including GE, IBM, and Facebook. [1]

At first glance, the story of Khazen Baz, an Arab woman and digital entrepreneur, might seem quite unique. However, as the most recent Global Entrepreneurship Monitor report indicates, such entrepreneurial stories are now increasingly coming from all parts of the world.[2] Indeed, the total *early-stage entrepreneurial activity*—measured as the proportion of adults who are actively engaged in starting or running

new businesses—has been increasing consistently in most parts of
the world. While the intensity of growth varies from one country to
another (e.g., within Latin America, Brazil has seen more growth than
Columbia and Mexico), the emerging broader picture is unmistak-
ably one of upward trending entrepreneurial activity across the world.
Importantly, a majority of start-ups in the world (especially those in the
tech sector) engage in at least one cross-border activity, rendering them
global ventures.[3]

Several factors—ranging from the availability of efficient global
supply chains to the preponderance of global consumer culture—
potentially explain this favorable trend in global entrepreneurship. At
the same time, as in the case of Khazen Baz and her Nabbesh, digitization is an important, and likely the most crucial, factor.

Digital technologies have made a profound impact on both the nature
and process of entrepreneurship; indeed, a separate field, called *digital
entrepreneurship*, has emerged to study their impact.[4] For example, digital crowdfunding platforms allow entrepreneurs to access funds from
investors from across the world. Digital technology-based tools such as
3D printing and VR allow entrepreneurs to build and test their products
at low cost. Global digital e-commerce platforms such as Amazon and
Alibaba provide entrepreneurs with instant access to global markets.
Social media platforms allow entrepreneurs to directly connect with
their global customers and to build their brands inexpensively. Cloud
computing, mobile computing, data analytics, and other digital technologies enable new ventures to scale up their global operations rapidly
and relatively risk-free. Together, all of these technologies have helped
to lower the barriers to venturing, allowing a greater number and more
diverse set of people from both developed and developing economies
to engage in international entrepreneurship—in effect, democratizing
global entrepreneurship.[5]

Recognizing the power of the digital economy to fuel entrepreneurship and growth, a number of countries have invested in digital infrastructures and adopted explicit policies to promote entrepreneurship.
The nature and scope of these national and regional initiatives and

measures are, of course, quite varied. For example, in September 2019, the Chinese government issued new guidelines for enhancing IP rights protection to strengthen the institutional environment of entrepreneurship in the country. Germany launched its Digital Hub Initiative in late 2018 to drive the country's transformation into a digital technology base, focused largely on start-ups. In 2019, the Jordanian government created the Ministry of Digital Economy and Entrepreneurship to stimulate digital entrepreneurship. The Indian government launched its National Innovation and Startup Policy 2019 program to enable educational institutions to actively engage students, faculties, and staff in innovation and entrepreneurship-related activities.

In parallel to such national policies, entrepreneurial ecosystems have been established in many regions of the world to bring together different stakeholders in the start-up world. These ecosystems play a critical role in educating/mentoring would-be entrepreneurs in start-up processes and in facilitating networking and resource sharing. Increasingly, such entrepreneurial ecosystems are founded on digital infrastructures, removing physical distance barriers or national border restrictions for entrepreneurs to access critical knowledge and ideas.[6]

The combination of powerful digital technologies and favorable digital policies and infrastructures has definitely enhanced the entrepreneurial capacity of different countries and led to the rapid growth of cross-border or global entrepreneurship. However, to really understand how digitization has enabled such cross-border entrepreneurship initiatives, we have to take a closer look at the different types of international entrepreneurial contexts. Indeed, a very diverse range of international new ventures is evident, all driven by digitization. While some are companies that use digital platforms to reach new foreign markets, others are digital natives: companies that simply would not exist without digital technologies and platforms.

In this chapter, we focus on three important digital global entrepreneurship contexts: (a) micro MNEs that leverage global digital market platforms, (b) digital-born globals that pursue accelerated internationalization, and (c) digitally-fueled international corporate entrepreneurship initiatives led by established multinationals. We discuss each of them and consider how their growth and success are also shaped by globalization and localization forces that exist in foreign markets. Through selected examples, we illustrate some of the strategies and practices successful digital global ventures have adopted. We start with micro MNEs.

Micro MNEs: Managing Dependencies on Digital Global Platforms

Micro MNEs are small companies that operate and market their products and services in multiple foreign markets. As economist Hal Varian noted, in the digital economy, micro MNEs combine the advantages of being small (the operational and market nimbleness that come with their relatively small size) with those of an established multinational (global access to markets and the ability to exploit global variations in skills and labor costs), leading to rapid growth and prominence.[7]

For many micro MNEs, the very basis of their existence is dependent on the plug-and-play services offered by global e-commerce platforms such as Amazon, Alibaba, JD.com, and eBay. At the same time, such overreliance on digital e-commerce platforms also creates dependencies that could stifle their continued growth and even survival.

Take the case of Chinese micro-MNEs that operate on Alibaba's Global Trade Services platform. Alibaba offers a plethora of services to micro MNEs through its various subsidiaries, including setting up dedicated "storefronts" on Tmall Global or Lazada, acquiring microloans from Ant Financial, communicating with and managing customer payments through Alipay, digital marketing through Alimama, and handling logistics and shipping through Cainiao. Once a micro MNE starts integrating all of its operations through these different services, to a great extent its fortunes are tied to the decisions made by Alibaba. As the CEO of one Chinese micro MNE told us, "When dealing with Alibaba's Global Trade Services, we really don't have any bargaining power in various terms of services and in revenue sharing . . . and often, to survive, our only option is to agree to all the conditions imposed."[8]

Micro MNEs are also exposed to the risks of operating in foreign markets that do not adhere to global business standards and policies. For example, sellers operating on Etsy to offer handcrafted products to foreign markets are susceptible to the theft of their intellectual property rights. Unlike established MNEs, they don't have the resources to pursue such issues legally, especially in distant markets where they have no physical presence. Such risks constitute another set of vulnerabilities for micro MNEs.

Thus, while digitization of the global business landscape has opened up a remarkable number of international expansion opportunities for micro MNEs, their ability to manage the risks posed by localization forces—whether in terms of the power of regional digital e-commerce platforms or the lack of appropriate IP regulations in target foreign markets—will shape their continued success.

One approach that micro MNEs have employed to address these challenges is to calibrate their platform dependency strategies on their growth phases. In general, during their early stages (say, the first few years of the venture), micro MNEs have more to gain from being closely embedded in or tightly coupled to a comprehensive digital market platform.

Consider the sellers on Etsy in India. As Himanshu Wardhan, who heads Esty in India, noted, Etsy's goal in India is "to attract and bring on board people who are creating or designing and making stuff at home and in small studios . . . we want to hold [their] hands and help them till the end . . . in order to create an Etsy shop and establish their business."[9] Most of Esty's sellers are first-time entrepreneurs, and as such their experience on the platform is an education in itself—on the basics of how to set up a business, export their wares, and manage all the associated paperwork, including taxes. To this end, Etsy launched a Discover India campaign that included conducting offline events on weekends and producing short videos, all designed to create awareness and to educate microentrepreneurs on the export potential offered by Etsy. The company also created a team of onboarding associates who would travel across the country and interact with the sellers (in-person and by phone). As Wardhan explained, they "become sort of consul-tants to these microentrepreneurs . . . they do not just help our sellers to set up a storefront or establish a PayPal account . . . they also advise them on basic business processes like inventory management . . . even helping them to optimize their shop so that they are set up for suc-cess."[10] All of this handholding becomes critical because for many of these microentrepreneurs, their very first sale is an export sale.

Many other e-commerce platforms also provide a similar portfolio of services that both educate microentrepreneurs and help micro MNEs establish their export businesses. For example, Booking.com offers a wide range of specialized online services that help small inns to not only to reach out to customers across the world but also automate and enhance the efficiency of their back-end operations, such as handling payments from foreign customers.

But as micro MNEs move beyond their early stages and gain some maturity in their businesses, the drawbacks related to their dependency on a single platform often tend to overcome the associated benefits. At that point, it makes increasing sense for micro MNEs to employ a greater degree of loose coupling with individual digital market plat-forms. Specifically, they can mix and match services offered by different e-commerce service providers—for example, combining the shipping system from one platform with the payment system from another platform—effectively using the plug-and-play flexibility offered by global digital market infrastructures. Another approach is to use digital e-commerce platforms promoted by industry associations and govern-ment agencies. For example, in India, the Federation of Indian Export Organizations (FEIO) has launched a cobranded digital platform called FEIO GlobalLinker, targeted at micro MNEs. It brings together a port-folio of e-commerce services offered by partners in different verticals (shipping and logistics, foreign exchange and banking, mobile connec-tivity, IP management, and digital marketing services).

Micro MNEs can also reduce IP risks and other related risks by exclusively targeting globalized markets, especially during their early growth stages. Such an approach allows a micro MNE to use favorable government policies and regulations in foreign markets to protect themselves in different ways when they are most vulnerable. As the founder of one Indian micro MNE in the apparel sector noted, "We initially focused exclusively on some of the large EU markets, although we used to get market queries from other regions including South America. . . . However, we have now gained enough confidence in our capabilities to use these digital platforms and do all the due diligence ourselves . . . and are now exploring opportunities in other [foreign] markets that are, let's say, much more challenging."[11] Importantly, a micro MNE's capability to do such due diligence is increasingly facilitated by digital technologies; for example, blockchain-based smart contracts can not only ensure transaction integrity but also enable smart IP rights management, indicating how micro MNEs can securely transition from globalized to localized markets by using appropriate digital infrastructures.[12]

More broadly, digitization allows micro MNEs to adapt or reorient their approach to different global e-commerce platforms and markets—from tightly to loosely coupled—so as to manage the risks associated with international expansion.

Digital Born Globals: Pursuing Sticky Business Models

Digital-born globals are companies that are not only born digital but also born global—that is, companies that are founded on digital technologies (in terms of their operations and/or offerings) and that pursue rapid internationalization from their inception. Examples of such digital-born globals abound in our economy today—from sharing economy companies such as Airbnb, Ola, and Uber to technology companies such as Netflix and Zoom.

A unique feature of digital-born globals is their reliance on a digitally infused or digitally enabled business model to rapidly gain a toehold in diverse foreign markets. As we noted in chapter 1, Airbnb, founded in 2008, expanded its operations into more than 191 countries in less than ten years, while Uber, launched in 2010, took only about eight years to establish a footprint in more than sixty-three countries. The portability of the underlying digitally enabled business model may help explain the rapid pace of their internationalization. At the same time, an overreliance on simply porting digital business models to new markets without taking into consideration unique aspects of the foreign market context could have considerable negative repercussions.

Remember OYO, the Indian hotel chain we briefly mentioned in the first chapter. Launched in 2013, it took only about six years for OYO to transform itself into one of the world's largest chains of leased and franchised hotels, homes, and managed living and work spaces. Before COVID-19, the company was valued at around $10 billion, had a presence in more than eight hundred cities in eighteen countries around the word (including in India, Malaysia, the UAE, China, Brazil, the UK, the Philippines, Japan, Saudi Arabia, Sri Lanka, Indonesia, Vietnam, and the United States), and was opening up new venues globally at a tearing pace of one hotel a day. However, a large part of OYO's international growth was fueled not necessarily by the uniqueness of its digital business model but unlimited speculative investments from SoftBank and other global venture capital firms.[13]

The company seemed not to have paid sufficient attention to the critical aspects of the foreign markets it was entering that determine the long-term sustainability or stickiness of the business model (how the business model is embedded in a local context), including local cultural issues. For example, in the past couple of years, the company has faced a host of complaints and lawsuits from its hotel partners in different countries, which are questioning the tenability of its partner relationships. As digital-born globals internationalize rapidly, their foreign partner relationships and their cultural underpinnings often assume greater significance than the innovative digital technologies themselves as such cultural ties may determine how "sticky" the business model is in that market. And in the post-COVID-19 world, OYO has had to retreat from some foreign markets, indicating how decoupled its business model was from the local contexts in these markets.

The same can be said about Uber's experience in some Asian markets. For example, one of the reasons Ola, Uber's home-grown Indian competitor, has been able to overtake Uber is the attention it has paid to the needs and behaviors of consumers in India, Singapore, Australia, and other countries in the region (e.g., consumer preferences for particular modes of payment). Similarly, Uber's lack of attention to local laws and regulations has arguably limited the pace of its expansion in several foreign markets, including Australia and the UK.

Digital technologies are highly flexible in their scope and scale of deployment, rendering the underlying business models of digital-born globals quite amenable to change. Indeed, the affordances (or action possibilities)[14] offered by digital technologies enable digital-born globals to adapt their business models and services to fit within the particular context of a foreign market without losing overall coherence. However, effective utilization of such digital technology affordances requires a keen understanding of the foreign market context—from relevant government policies and regulations to digital/business infrastructures to business/consumer culture. In other words, it is the nature of the coupling between the digital born globals' business model and the foreign market context that will determine the stickiness of the business model and thereby the long-term success of the business.

Digital-born globals can pursue tight coupling if the central assumptions of their business models—in terms of laws and regulations, infrastructure, and culture—align well with the prevailing conditions of a foreign market. For example, much of the early internationalization success of streaming giant Netflix has been predicated on this—especially in North American and EU markets. One such assumption is unquestioned access to and free riding on local communication networks in foreign markets. However, when that assumption becomes questionable, it can raise a host of challenges for the company. For instance, in South Korea, lawmakers considered changes to the country's Telecommunications Business Act in order to regulate global content providers' free access to local networks so that global companies such as Netflix could no longer cause traffic explosions and enjoy enormous profits without sharing the network expansion and upgrade costs.[15] Netflix's ability to adapt to such localization forces and employ loose coupling

in certain foreign markets may decide the continued success of its foreign expansion plans. To a certain extent, Netflix has already demon-
strated such adaptation capability. During the COVID-19 crisis, when
streaming volumes increased exponentially in many foreign markets,
Netflix started reducing the streaming quality in some markets, including Europe, India, and Australia, so as to reduce the company's impact
on internet speeds there.

More broadly, while digitization may facilitate and drive digital-born
globals' rapid internationalization plans, their continued success will
be shaped by how well they adapt their business models and operations
to changing globalization and localization forces present in different
foreign markets. Companies that turn a blind eye to the power of such
contextual forces and rely only on throwing more and more money at
their global expansion plans are doomed to fail.

International Corporate Venturing: Sensing and Seizing Boundary-Crossing Opportunities

The third context for global entrepreneurship is corporate venturing
initiatives pursued by established, large multinationals. Corporate venturing has always been an important vehicle for rapid growth for multinationals, but digitization has transformed companies' capabilities in
two significant ways.

First, digital global business connectivity has enhanced the speed
with which MNEs can sense and seize new opportunities in distant
foreign markets. A key advantage of an MNE that has a physical presence in different parts of the world is the ability to sense and combine market-related signals coming from digital sources (social media)
and nondigital sources (physical stores, suppliers, manufacturing units,
personal interactions with government regulators). But without digital technologies, many of these signals acquired over space and time
are processed separately in different parts of a company, leading to a
loss of market-related insights. With the deployment of data analytic
technologies, including AI, it has become possible for multinationals

to channel all such information into one place and to consider them together.

Consider Unilever, which operates in more than 190 countries worldwide. The company has set up around thirty "people data centers" in different parts of the world, each of which brings together diverse types of market data (structured and unstructured) from multiple internal and external sources—for example, social media data, call center data, CRM data, local consumer reports, local manager reports, and so on. The company then utilizes a suite of AI and data analytics solutions to integrate all these data and generate market insights that highlight new business opportunities in specific regional and local markets. Some of these insights may relate to placing existing products in new markets, but other insights imply totally new market possibilities.

What is striking, however, is the diversity of data used and the speed with which customer insights are generated. As we mentioned briefly in chapter 3, in one case, the company combined AI-based metaphor analysis of Indian (Bollywood) film songs with internal market data for the ice cream product category to make a connection between ice cream and breakfast that quickly led to the discovery of a new market opportunity.

There are vast amounts of all types of unstructured data available on consumer perceptions and desires (e.g., via social media interactions), but what is often a key capability in large companies is the empathy for the consumer in a specific region that is needed to make sense of that data and make the critical connection to a market opportunity. As Stan Sthanunathan, Unilever's head of consumer and market insights, noted, "People have learned to sympathize but not empathize with consumers . . . and strangely enough AI and machine learning are actually beginning to fill that role."[16] In the past couple of years, such techniques have allowed Unilever to generate a number of key market insights that have in turn opened up several novel business development opportunities across the world.

The second way digitization has shaped corporate venturing is by allowing multinationals to cross the boundaries of their existing industries and move into new markets with the same internal assets. In short, digitization has made industry boundary crossing easier in international markets. As we noted in an earlier chapter, digital assets are highly modularized and can be combined with other assets and deployed in diverse contexts to serve different purposes. This versatility inherent in digital assets allows multinationals to quickly pursue promising opportunities in industries and markets that are outside their current portfolio. Further, as the infusion of digital assets in products and services continue to increase, such boundary-crossing, international venturing opportunities will become available to companies in all types of industries and markets.

A case in point is DJI, the Chinese drone manufacturer that has quickly become the world leader in creating and marketing consumer unmanned aerial vehicles. Its success lies in its creative use, design, and integration of technologies and global open resources in aerial imaging, autopilot, camera stabilization, remote control, data storage and transmission, GPS, vision sensors, and videography. Most of these technologies are digital or have digital components. In pursuing diverse market opportunities, DJI was focused on partnering with other companies to integrate its digital assets and competencies with those of others. For example, it teamed up with Berkeley-based 3D Robotics for developing advanced business-focused drones. It acquired Swedish high-end camera company Hasselblad for new imaging technologies. Similarly, it partnered with San Francisco–based Skycatch to develop industrial drones for Japanese multinational Komatsu. That initiative involved combining DJI's Matrice 100 enterprise drone platform (hardware) with Skycatch's high-precision and 3D technologies for aerial surveying (software). Through innovative design, creative integration, and modular production, DJI makes these complex technologies into simplified, easy-to-use, and cost-efficient products that serve mass global markets for consumers, professionals, and enterprises. More broadly, DJI did not create or invent most of the technologies; rather, its unique entrepreneurial focus has been on understanding how to mix and match different technological assets to cater to emergent opportunities in different types of drone markets, some industrial and some consumer-oriented, and in different geographical regions.

Thus, though digital technologies have enhanced established multinationals' connectivity with foreign customers, partners, and resources, their success in international venturing will depend on their ability to use those technologies to generate (and act upon) highly contextualized market insights that reflect the peculiarities related to local consumer culture and preferences, business regulations and practices, and digital infrastructure.

Conclusion

Digitization has worked wonders for the pursuit of entrepreneurship—both domestically and globally, and for all types of entrepreneurs, from first-time entrepreneurs to established firms. Digitization has not only lowered the costs and risks of venturing but also enhanced the speed with which it could be pursued internationally. But globalization and localization forces can critically contextualize the success parameters of such international entrepreneurship. In this chapter, our focus has been to bring your attention to this perspective and the underlying issues, particularly in the case of micro MNEs, digital-born globals, and MNE corporate ventures.

Our discussion so far points to three key takeaways:

1. *Micro MNEs can calibrate their digital platform strategies during their growth or life cycle stages,* making themselves more tightly coupled to a comprehensive digital market platform during their early life stages and more loosely coupled to multiple digital market platforms once they gain some maturity in their business.

2. *Digital-born globals can ensure the stickiness of their business model in an international market* (and thereby the long-term success of the business) by utilizing digital technology affordances and achieving the right degree of coupling (tight or loose) between their business model and the market context (globalized or localized).

3. *Established multinationals can pursue international venturing by utilizing their digital global business connectivity to quickly sense and seize novel boundary-crossing opportunities*, by generating and acting on highly contextualized market insights that reflect the distinctiveness of specific countries or regions.

More broadly, entrepreneurs and companies have to carefully consider localization forces evident in different foreign markets and adapt their business models and business strategies accordingly. Otherwise, digital forces are going to take them only so far in their global entrepreneurship efforts.

In the next chapter, we consider some of the risks associated with the digitization of international business.

9 Managing Risks in Digital Global Business

So far, we have considered how digital global business connectivity—based on new and powerful digital technologies—affords novel opportunities and capabilities that multinationals can employ to pursue international expansion in both globalized and localized markets. While we did mention briefly, here and there, the risks associated with such digital global business connectivity, we have not examined them in detail. In this chapter, we focus on the "dark side" of digital global business connectivity and, more broadly, that of digitization of international business.

From Intracountry Risks to Extracountry Risks

The risks arising from digitization in the global business context fall into two broad groups: (a) intracountry risks that relate to risks in a specific country and (b) extracountry risks that relate to risks that reach beyond one particular country.[1] We first briefly consider the different risk categories in each of these groups and then discuss in more detail a few specific types of risks that assume added significance in the context of digital global business connectivity.

Intracountry risks include regulatory risks, infrastructure risks, economic risks, and social risks.

Regulatory risks relate to policy restrictions or deterrence by governments on digital connectivity and digital commerce, discrimination against foreign firms' access to digital infrastructure, regulatory uncertainty and ambiguity regarding data security and data privacy, promonopoly policies, and abrupt changes in governmental rules. Other important regulatory risks include weak intellectual property rights protection and poor transparency in formulating and enforcing economic policies toward digitization.

Infrastructure risks relate to a myriad set of physical conditions in a country's digital infrastructure that shape the quality of digitization and exert a massive impact on multinationals' ability to operate in that country. These include broadband supply (fiber optics, 4G or 5G coverage), internet bandwidth, mobile telecommunications, data centers, cloud computing infrastructure, and IoT infrastructure.

Economic risks comprise a country's overall economic soundness and the advancement of key economic sectors related to digitization (e.g., electronics, computing, software, robotics). The country's demand size, openness to digital products and services, and internet penetration and usage are also economic items that significantly impact a multinational's global digital business connectivity in a host country.

Social risks relate to a host country's social conditions—including social unrest, violence, crime, population dynamics, and income inequity—that could hinder multinationals' initiatives to expand operations in that country. Changing consumer culture and social norms and behaviors (in perceiving, receiving, and consuming digital products and services) could also pose risks to multinationals.

Extracountry risks include those that arise from global geopolitics, home-host country ties, and international events.

As we have seen in the last few years, *global geopolitics* can generate formidable and unpredictable risks for multinationals as digitization quickens the spillover of global geopolitical tensions and uncertainty into international business. Amid an increasing number of trade disputes between countries, the scrutiny by many governments of takeovers by foreign companies has increased, with a sharper focus on the implications for national security and technological advantages associated with digital technologies and infrastructures. For example, in Europe, the economic collapse that followed the COVID-19 pandemic made many companies very attractive targets for foreign acquisition. Subsequently, many EU member countries (including Germany, France, Poland, and Spain) adopted stricter regulation of foreign investments and takeovers—particularly Chinese acquisitions—in response to national security concerns.[2]

Home-host country ties can also pose considerable risks for multinationals as worsened bilateral relationships between home and host countries (or regions) can translate into greater friction in international business. Again, as recent events in the United States, the UK, India, and China have shown, even minor issues in bilateral ties can inflame consumer sentiments and make them less favorable for foreign multinationals.

International events—ranging from pandemics and other natural disasters to terrorism, cyberattacks, and other human-induced disasters—pose important risks for multinationals as they impede or disrupt international business structures and processes. While digital global business connectivity could help multinationals cope with some of these disasters (as evidenced by how companies adapted to COVID-19 by shifting to work-at-home structures), their unpredictability and scope could still contribute to the fragility of multinationals' businesses. Similarly, digital technologies have made it easier for criminal groups or individuals to conduct foreign assaults, in secret or by proxy. Further, attacks on multinationals' digital networks by entities connected with foreign governments have become increasingly frequent in recent years. For example, the US Justice Department recently alleged that a group of hackers associated with China's main intelligence service had infiltrated more than one hundred businesses to steal data.[3]

All of these broad categories of risks are relevant to some extent in the digital global business context, but ahead we identify five specific risks that together characterize digital global business connectivity risks: interdependence risks, information security risks, international reputation fragility, new global rivals, and institutional and infrastructural risks (see figure 9.1).

Interdependence Risks

Digital globalization makes international companies more dependent on others and thus subject to more contagious effects from all risks facing them and others. A more interconnected, digital world magnifies the impact of external shocks and spreads ripple effects faster. The 2008 financial crisis showed how rapidly linkages between the world's capital markets can allow contagion to spread.[4] The globalization of financial systems and the acceleration of information transmission have increased the risk of financial crises: a crisis in one country can spread to others and lead to worldwide crises. The US-China trade war makes such interdependence risks even greater. Further, as we have found in the COVID-19 crisis, redesigning and relocating global supply chains are very costly and cumbersome tasks for most multinationals. For example, because today's digital business infrastructure (e.g., robotic process automation, AI-supported inventory algorithms) is critical for global production networks and supply chains, many US and European firms are finding it difficult to quickly relocate their operations to other emerging markets that can substitute for China's supply base. In the long run, an important remedy and precaution is not just to relocate the supply chain to another country but also to regionalize (localize) and diversify the supplier base, avoiding overreliance on a few suppliers or distributors and from a single foreign country. At the same time, local government regulations and employee unions in different geographical locations may pose another set of constraints as companies start tackling this issue.

Information Security Risks

As digital commerce becomes the default in most industries (particularly as a consequence of COVID-19), multinationals are becoming extremely dependent on the exchange of information across the internet. And as information flows across national borders, the concern for data security grows: business transaction data collected by international companies are no longer safe once they are transmitted via the internet or any other public digital network. Global internet breaches can

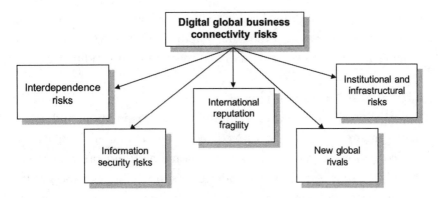

Figure 9.1
Digitization risks in international business

disable enterprise system infrastructure or pilfer confidential information such as customer credit card numbers, social security numbers, and business transactions. As more people shop online, more opportunities arise for businesses to collect personal data and for hackers to steal that info. The indirect damage from such breaches can be considerable and difficult to recover from and can include the loss of consumer trust and business reputation. Thus information security threats and cyberattacks arise as a new type of international risk for virtually all multinationals.

High-profile hacks and breaches have already hit many of the world's largest companies. One report notes that cybercrime, including consumer data breaches, financial crimes, market manipulation, and theft of intellectual property, cost the global economy about $600 billion in 2017, and this figure ballooned to $1 trillion in 2018, indicating the seriousness of information security risks.[5] The US Department of Homeland Security and the Federal Bureau of Investigation reported that hackers linked to Russian government operatives have attacked American firms in a variety of sectors, including energy, water, aviation, and manufacturing, while the United States reportedly hacked the Russian grid. Similarly, the NotPetya attack in 2017, a virus targeting Ukrainian government agencies and businesses, spread to various multinational corporations. It caused an estimated $870 million in losses for Merck; $400 million for FedEx's European subsidiary TNT Express; $300 million to Maersk, a Danish shipping giant; and $188 million to Mondelez, which makes many popular snack foods, including Oreos.[6]

International Reputation Fragility

Digital globalization makes a multinational's reputation and crisis management immensely sensitive and fragile. A company's *reputation* is a collection of perceptions and opinions, past and present, about the organization, and this collection resides in the consciousness of its stakeholders. Global reputation stands as perhaps the most important intangible asset that directly affects the market value of a multinational firm. Contagion effects that jeopardize the multinational's worldwide reputation due to its corporate or executive wrongdoing multiply through social media and other digital connectivity channels.

The demise of a few companies can engulf a whole industry when the transactions are based on trust in the fulfilment of future promises. For example, consider the tax-shaming scandal in the UK involving some leading US multinationals, including Google, Amazon, and Starbucks. Amazon reported UK sales of £3.35 billion in 2011, but only paid £1.8 million in tax. Meanwhile, Google's ad unit paid just £6 million to HM Treasury in 2011 despite a UK turnover of £395 million. Although their actions were legal, ramifications included a huge negative impact on the tide of public opinion.[7] And in this age of social media influencers, the effects of such public shaming can reverberate for a long time, affecting a multinational's future international expansion plans. Similarly, the emergence of fake news and deliberate spreading of unsubstantiated news or misinformation about a company via social media can seriously and rapidly damage corporate reputation. As Warren Buffet, CEO of Berkshire Hathaway, wisely noted, "It takes twenty years to build a reputation and five minutes to destroy it."[8] Digital global business connectivity significantly enhances and accelerates the adverse spreading of a company scandal across the globe and makes multinationals' reputations much more fragile.

New Global Rivals

Digitization, a driver of next-generation competition, adds flexibility to but also accelerates and redefines the dynamics of competition. Traditional definitions of *an industry* are becoming outdated as digitization drives convergence across numerous formerly separate realms of value-creation activity. Digitization also fosters the emergence and growth of many new types of global rivals, especially those building on digital platforms that cross industry boundaries. Despite their smallness or newness, these new global players prove to be fast and agile, often adopting a connectivity-enabled business model that allows them to appropriate new and fitted customer value propositions for highly localized markets.

Unlike traditional competition, wherein firms know their local and international rivals well, global competition today is characterized by the rapid rise of a large number of small businesses and digital-born globals that multinationals may not even take notice of until it's too late. For instance, in healthcare, AI-based start-ups such as Bay Labs, AliveCor, CrossChx, and Prognos are all now potent rivals to long-established large multinationals such as Philips Healthcare. Similarly, digital, mobile-only banks, such as Monzo and Revolut, have signed up millions of customers in recent years, prompting big and traditional multinationals to modernize their services and, in some cases, build entirely new bank brands to compete (as HSBC did with its new First Direct division in the UK).

Institutional and Infrastructural Risks

Multinationals need to decipher a new type of risk not only from a digital/physical infrastructure standpoint but also from an institutional perspective. To make digital global business strategies work, multinationals depend on easy access to cohesive, current, and flexible infrastructures in foreign markets. Infrastructural risks can arise from three sources: emergence of siloed digital infrastructures, or *splinternet*; disruptions of digital infrastructure that occur due to various reasons; and the unpredictability of changes in rules and policies that govern multi-nationals' access and usage.

First, as we discussed in the first two chapters, there is increasing concern in many countries about becoming too reliant on the digital infrastructures owned and operated by a few dominant countries—that is, concern about *digital colonization*. For example, very few countries outside the United States currently have the ability to build massive cloud infrastructures, which are the backbones for everything digital. In response, many countries are either developing new regulations and policies for where multinationals can store their data (cloud locations) or investing in their own dedicated national digital infrastructures that are to a certain extent delinked from the internet. All of these changes pose important risks for multinationals in terms of their access to a worldwide digital infrastructure, as well as their ability to move data around to make the best use of it.

Second, as we have seen from the COVID-19 crisis, when disruptions of physical and institutional infrastructures for digital global business connectivity unfold, there will be severe and widespread consequences for multinationals all along the global and digital value chain. A recent report ranked various countries on the robustness of their key digital platforms (e-commerce, digital media, etc.) and the resilience of their internet infrastructure against traffic surges.[9] In general, advanced economies scored high on robustness of digital platforms compared to developing economies, but when it came to resilience of internet infrastructure, there was wide disparity even among the developed economies. For example, countries such as the United States, Germany, Canada, and Singapore scored high on infrastructure resilience, but many others, including Japan, Sweden, Italy, China, and France, did not, indicating that multinationals have to carefully evaluate not just the quality of the digital platforms in a country but also the quality of the underlying infrastructure.

Third, the breadth and depth of infrastructural regulations and policies has been continually increasing, in developed and develop-ing countries, with additional scrutiny on areas such as customer data protection, digital taxes, information security, and national security. Further, the institutional and infrastructural environment for digital global business connectivity comprises numerous players, aside from the national governments that enact policymaking, regulations, standard setting, and investment in digital infrastructure. For example, these players include supranational agencies such as the International Telecommunication Union (ITU) and the World Wide Web Consortium, as well as industry associations, communications service providers, and hardware and software manufacturers. The dynamics associated with all these players, their diverse motivations and influence, enhance the overall unpredictability of the attendant infrastructural risks in a foreign market.

Beyond all these, informal institutions—socially shared, usually unwritten rules created, communicated, and enforced outside formal institutions—can also shape the success of digital global businesses and thus hold considerable risks. Social behaviors and consumption norms in target foreign countries signify important factors that global businesses should consider in assessing risks. For instance, eBay failed in China largely because of an insufficient understanding of China's unique social and consumption conduct, called *swift guanxi* (personalized and long-term relationship building with consumers). But its lead rival, Taobao, understood the dynamics well enough. It incorporated elements in its platform that enabled such a culture through instant messaging, promoting personalized interactions between seller and buyer. As such, multinationals also need to carefully assess the risks that may arise from an incomplete understanding of the informal institutions pertaining to a foreign market.

Table 9.1 offers a simple twenty-item, five-point scale to evaluate the aggregate digital global business connectivity risk for a multinational. As the table indicates, the total score across all twenty items in the scale (which will range from 20 to 100) can provide a good idea of the overall risk profile of a company. For example, a total score that is 80 or above would imply a prohibitively high-risk environment for the multinational and the need for aggressive measures to mitigate it. In the rest of

Table 9.1
Scale to evaluate digital global business connectivity risks

Risk category		Survey items	Not true at all			Very true		Risk Score
			1	2	3	4	5	
Interdependency risks	1	Many of our partners are located in countries that have frequent conflict with our home country.						
	2	Our key global operations and activities (e.g., supply chain, technologies) are highly concentrated in certain countries.						
	3	We depend on third-party digital platforms and cloud providers without much control.						
	4	Our global operations are geographically dispersed yet digitally intermingled tightly.						
Information security risks	1	My company operates in countries and regions that have very little capability to resist cyberattacks.						
	2	Our major foreign partners are highly susceptible to (or have a history of experiencing) cyberattacks.						
	3	A lot of our business data (transactions) flow over the public internet or third-party cloud infrastructure.						
	4	As part of our operations, our business data frequently cross national borders.						
International reputation fragility	1	Our customers frequently talk about my company on social media and other public digital forums.						
	2	My company is situated in an industry that has a history of public relation disasters.						

Table 9.1 (continued)

Risk category		Survey items	Not true at all				Very true	Risk Score
			1	2	3	4	5	
	3	We use global, rather than localized, brand(s) for our products and services in foreign operations.						
	4	Our global customers are quite sensitive to the consistency and coherence of our company's/product's reputation across countries.						
New global rivals	1	My industry has seen the emergence of new rivals that use digital technologies to offer novel value propositions in the markets in which we compete.						
	2	My company is highly susceptible to rivals from adjacent industries and markets.						
	3	Rapid digitization of business models has led to many new international ventures in our industry and adjacent industries.						
	4	Many medium and small businesses in various countries use global e-commerce platforms to compete against us.						
Institutional and infrastructural risks	1	We operate in countries that are setting up their own national digital infrastructures that are not tightly integrated with the global internet.						
	2	We operate in countries that have established stringent and restrictive policies regarding cross-border data flows and local data storage.						

Table 9.1 (continued)

Risk category	Survey items	Not true at all				Very true	Risk Score
		1	2	3	4	5	
	3 We operate in countries that are subject to highly intricate and opaque regulations and policies related to digital taxation, information security, and digital infrastructure access.						
	4 We operate in countries that have informal institutions (e.g., business cultures) that are distinctly different from those of our home country.						

Note: Aggregate risk score is as follows: 20–39, *low risk*; 40–59, *moderate risk*; 60–79, *high risk*; 80–100, *prohibitive risk*.

this chapter, we discuss how multinationals can continually assess and manage the different types of digitization risks.

Approaches to Assess Digital Global Business Connectivity Risks

Digital infrastructure refers to foundational services that define the communication and digital technology capabilities of a nation, region, city, or organization. The elements of such digital infrastructure range from internet data routes, IoT, mobile telecommunications networks, and cloud computing data centers to digital platforms, applications, and user devices. Multinationals need to assess the availability, quality, cost, speed, convenience, and upgrading of such digital infrastructure in a foreign market as it critically shapes their ability to reach out to customers and expand their operations in that market.

One approach is to rely on country-level risk ratings provided by different international agencies. For example, the Global Connectivity Index rates around eighty nations on their digital infrastructure and provides a ranking that allows multinationals to quickly assess and compare the overall quality and potential of digital infrastructure in different foreign markets.[10] Global Connectivity Index ratings use a set of forty indicators that capture both supply-side and demand-side digital infrastructure components, as well as the current level of and future potential for key technology enablers (information and communications technology [ICT]fundamentals, broadband, data centers, cloud, AI/big data, and IoT).

Such country-level ratings are useful to get a quick overview of the extent of risks in a foreign market, but often international business managers need to go beyond that and assess the extent of specific types of digitization risks (at least for their companies' major foreign markets). Both qualitative and quantitative approaches can be used for this purpose. We describe a few such methods here that are appropriate for assessing digital global business connectivity risks.

Qualitative approaches involve employing a substantial amount of expert insights, judgmental inputs, and subjective analysis.

The *grand tour approach* relies on on-the-field company intelligence. A multinational may dispatch a team of specialists (such as those from IT, the global supply chain, marketing, or other areas) to work together with its foreign subsidiary specialists in order to identify and analyze the digitization risk situation and offer potential solutions and remedies. This method allows the company to adapt its corporate risk analysis framework to the specific risks relevant in a foreign market.

The *old hands approach* relies on seasoned external experts coming from intelligence, consulting, academic, and digital technology communities, as well as from industry networks. These experts can help bring insights from peer firms and related industries to a specific foreign market in order to analyze the digitalization-related uncertainties and challenges and translate them into a digital global business connectivity risk assessment for the multinational's operations in that market.

The *checklist approach* involves conducting due diligence, coordinated by a headquarters team composed of experts from related functions and areas (such as internal control, risk assessment, digital technologies, global planning, crisis management, supply chain, and the like). The checklist usually requires questions and items to be thoroughly assessed and sequential steps to be implemented as planned. To tackle digital globalization risks, this checklist technique can be employed on a periodic basis for routine assessment of risks, as well as on a nonperiodic basis to address a sudden outbreak of new risks occurring in a specific foreign subsidiary or with the MNE's global operations more broadly.

The *power link approach* assumes a series of linkages among social, political, and environmental changes that lead to an upheaval in digitization risks, as discussed earlier. This approach first requires a careful identification of the main factors and causes driving these linkages (e.g., trade-related tensions between home and host countries). This approach also requires a detailed analysis of the structures of power links to identify influence circles. These power circles then are examined to find their relative strength, evolution and trajectory, and impact on business prospects, and finally, optimal solutions to tackle them are investigated.

Qualitative approaches are handicapped by their inability to reveal, longitudinally, comparatively, and consistently, the level or amount of digitization risks. Quantitative techniques arise to fill this void and meet analytical needs, especially for multinational enterprises highly exposed to such risks.

Under the quantitative approach, digitization risk measures are usually tabulated and analyzed by techniques such as integrated computer modeling and simulation, AI/machine learning, and complexity analytics, among others. With diverse types of big data becoming available for analysis—data from the multinational's own internal operations, ecosystem partners, and the broader industry environment—these modern data analytics techniques can be employed to identify and assess risk patterns that link economic, social, political, and other dimensions. Importantly, such quantitative methods allow multinationals to monitor and analyze risks and associated behaviors/activities in real time and for globally dispersed activities inside and outside the multinational.

For example, AI-based risk analytics platforms, a component of the quantitative approach, can assess global supply chain risks by integrating various types of information about suppliers—from their geographical and geopolitical environments to their financial risk, sustainability, and corporate social responsibility scores.[11] Similarly, AI-based algorithms can be trained to assess cybersecurity risks by linking operational data such as financial transactions with other behavioral information, such as email traffic, calendar items, office building check-in and check-out times, and even telephone calls. It should be noted, however, that some of these approaches may raise important issues related to employee privacy rights.

Qualitative and quantitative methods can be combined in different ways to create different types of digital global business connectivity risk-assessment systems—from early warning systems to early learning systems that prevent threats from materializing.

Improving Digital Infrastructures as a Way to Curb Digitization Risks

One way to reduce digitization risks is to improve the quality and scope of physical and institutional digital infrastructures in a country, and this rests on the shoulders of the respective governments, the private sector (including multinationals), and other players, such as international economic organizations (the WTO, the World Bank, the Organisation for Economic Co-operation and Development [OECD], and the International Monetary Fund [IMF]), sustainability nongovernmental organizations (NGOs), and industry associations.

Governments themselves need to innovate on their digital infrastructure, shifting more administrative and public services online and onto mobile phones. Digital connectivity offers huge advantages in terms of administrative efficiency, resilience, and ubiquity of access for all citizens. A good illustration of this is the Digital India initiative launched by the Indian government in 2015. Its goal was to transform the country into a digitally empowered society and knowledge economy by developing secure and stable digital infrastructure, delivering a greater number of government services digitally, and ensuring the digital literacy of all citizens.[12] In the last few years, the initiative has helped to spur considerable investments in connecting rural areas with high-speed internet networks. Although the ostensible benefits of such an initiative are for the country's citizens and the government, it also helps the private sector by developing a huge market that can be accessed digitally. Indeed, a number of foreign multinationals have made decisions to expand their operations in India based on this initiative. The country's e-commerce market has been growing at an annualized rate of about 13 percent, but the COVID-19 pandemic turned out to be an inflection point; the number of users engaged in digital commerce increased exponentially in just the first two quarters of 2020.[13]

Individual governments also need to foster contributions by and collaboration with the private sector, including companies from foreign countries, to enhance their digital infrastructures. For example, governments could create a procompetition, transparent policy setting that helps drive private investment and innovation for digital infrastructure. Creative solutions, like coinvestment via public-private partnerships, should also be facilitated for this purpose.

Multinational enterprises can also play a key role in improving digital infrastructure directly, which in turn nurtures their global expansion. A number of technology companies have done so both on the upstream side of the infrastructure (Cisco, Samsung, Ericsson, NEC, NTT, Vodafone, Reliance, Verizon, Hitachi, Wipro and Telefonica) and on the downstream side (Amazon, Alibaba, eBay, JD.com, Facebook, YouTube). Many other multinationals, such as Sony, 3Com, Google, Panasonic, TCL, Fujitsu, and Toshiba, to name a few, have also supported global connectivity by providing digitization technologies. Government actions that appear to discriminate against foreign investors will cause such companies to take their investments elsewhere and make it difficult to attract new investors. At the same time, digital sovereignty concerns are clouding government decisions about which foreign companies will be allowed to invest in a country's digital infrastructures.

Managerial Approaches to Curb Digitization Risks

Although there are no easy solutions to mitigating digital global business connectivity risks, multinationals can adopt a few broad strategies to equip themselves with the capabilities to both detect an emergent business risk from a foreign market and respond to it in ways that reduce its impact on their business operations in that market and elsewhere. Here, we consider three such managerial approaches.

The first relates to multinationals' data and digital technology architectures and strategies. As mentioned previously, the complexity of the emerging digital global business context implies that simplistic risk-analysis techniques that rely on analyzing different data in isolation are unlikely to be sufficient. Fortunately, powerful AI-based techniques (from machine learning to natural language processing) are now available that can jointly analyze different types of data pertaining to different aspects of a multinational's business to decipher emergent risks. In other words, data, analytics, and digital technology architectures have become the key enablers for multinationals' risk management. Highly fragmented digital and data architectures cannot provide an efficient or effective framework for international business risk management. Instead, multinationals will need to adopt data and digital technology architectures across the enterprise that sensitize them to weak signals or emerging threats, emanating from subsidiaries in different foreign markets, that may soon disrupt global operations in a significant manner. More broadly, multinationals' data/digital architectures should allow for building both local intelligence (pertaining to emerging risks in specific foreign markets) and global intelligence (pertaining to emerging risks from global events) and for their joint consideration to understand the scope and pattern of the overall risks.

Another set of strategies relates to preparing the enterprise in terms of structural arrangements to decipher and adapt to emergent risks. In an earlier chapter, we gave the example of Haier, a Chinese white goods giant. Haier restructured its entire organization by creating thousands of microenterprises, each of which operates independently in developing products and services for the smart home.[14] Such a structure helps to reduce the distance between the employees and end users (a concept captured by the term *Ren Dan He Yi* or *unity of people and order*) and sensitizes the entire organization to weak signals of risks emanating from different parts of the world. Another related approach is to invest in training risk-management staff in both the headquarters and subsidiaries, allowing them to apply their digital skillsets in their day-to-day activities in order to predict digital disruptions, provide actionable advices, and develop risk-mitigation solutions. In other words, it involves developing structural elements that bring together the data/digital architectures mentioned earlier and the employee skills that can leverage the same in order to identify and manage emerging risks. To this end, many multinationals, including Cisco, IBM, and SAP, have set up roaming *global digital risk squads*—cross-functional and cross-border teams formed from a variety of different disciplines and business units, responsible for managing both the technical/digital and commercial aspects of risks associated with core businesses or activities of the enterprise.

Finally, governance strategies, pertaining to external partners, also form an important component of digitization risk management. Chief among them is achieving the right level of governance, both initially and perpetually, on topics such as business continuity and data integrity and security. For example, it is advisable to reassess risk issues over time, such as whether or not the firm should depend on a single cloud provider in a foreign market or outsource a critical part of the customer journey to a single third party, or the extent of automation of core processes. Similarly, multinationals have to undertake adequate oversight of automation, whether through deployment of robotic process automation software or automating data flows between systems in an end-to-end customer journey. The critical task in all such efforts will be to set up an appropriate governance framework that defines accountability for data and processes spanning multiple partners, subsidiaries, and countries.

Conclusion

Globalization is entering a new era that is full of extreme disruptions and adversities—health and humanitarian crises, collapse of customer demand, antiglobalization sentiments, regulatory interference, supply chain breakdown, unemployment, and economic recession, to name a few—which heighten the risks of all types of cross-border business operations. Digital global business connectivity can help multinationals to better cope with such extreme disruptions, but they also need to adopt explicit strategies that will enhance their capabilities to both become aware of emergent threats and respond to them in a timely fashion.

Our discussion so far indicates two key takeaways:

1. A critical part of risk strategizing is *conducting a careful evaluation of the different types of global business risks.* Managers should ask themselves not only what their company's aggregate risk score is but also on what dimension the risk is greatest, so as to tailor their risk-management strategies.

2. Multinationals should *adopt a diverse set of digital global business connectivity risk management approaches*—from contributing to enhancing the quality of global/regional digital infrastructures to adopting novel structural arrangements and partner/ecosystem governance strategies.

It is also increasingly clear that beyond the management approaches described here, a multinational's overall *digital resilience*—its digitalization-enabled distinctive capabilities to anticipate, withstand, and rapidly recover from adverse events or hardships—will assume considerable significance in managing the risks inherent in global business. Indeed, such digital resilience will complement and enhance the value of the risk-management approaches discussed in this chapter.

But how does a company build digital resilience? That is the topic of our final chapter.

10 Digital Intelligence and Digital Resilience: Putting Digital Global Business Connectivity into Practice

We started this book by describing how two emergent forces—digital forces and regional/local forces—have radically redrawn the global business landscape with the potential to shape multinational companies' future performance and success in international expansion. When the two of us started the initial research for this book, the COVID-19 pandemic wasn't on the horizon. Even then, it was clear how rapidly these two forces were intensifying and how transformative they would be. New digital technologies such as IoT, AI, and blockchain had swept across the business world, promising a new era in how businesses create and how customers consume value. At the same time, a host of international issues that had been stewing for quite some time had boiled over—from Brexit to the US-China trade conflict—revealing the fault lines in the globalized business world.

The COVID-19 pandemic only further intensified or augmented both these forces. All evidence indicates that in about eight weeks' time (from March to April 2020), both businesses and consumers the world over vaulted forward in the use of digital technologies to an extent that otherwise would have taken them about three to five years to reach. And those fault lines in the global business world? Well, they are now deep and broad crevices, pointing to the diverse types of barriers that have emerged to hinder cross-border business and the increased significance of highly localized foreign markets.

Indeed, it wouldn't be unreasonable to conclude that these forces have now combined to create the *new normal* for global businesses.

Throughout this book, we advanced and elaborated on the concept of digital global business connectivity to help companies navigate this new global business landscape. Our discussion has focused on the different elements and strategies associated with the four dimensions of digital global business connectivity (table 10.1). But it is not sufficient for multinationals to focus on one or two of these dimensions or one or two international markets they operate in. Rather, they have to adopt an enterprise-wide view and consider the portfolio of strategies across the different dimensions of digital global business connectivity and across the different regions. Importantly, the different strategies that a multinational adopts need to not only coexist but also reinforce one another in helping it successfully operate in both globalized and localized international markets.

This is easier said than done. As the scope and the diversity of a multinational's international operations increase, it becomes increasingly complex and difficult to maintain such a coherent approach to digital global business connectivity. How should companies address this challenge?

Our answer—which forms the focus of this final chapter—is for enterprises to develop a set of digital technology–related capabilities. Specifically, we suggest that companies have to invest in and build employee-level *digital mindfulness*, team/business unit–level *digital intelligence*, and organization-level *digital resilience*. In this chapter, we define each of these enterprise capabilities and discuss how together they contribute to establishing and maintaining digital global business connectivity.

We conclude the chapter (and this book) by focusing on some of the core themes and practices that underlie digital global business connectivity—themes and practices that reflect the insights and the wisdom we distilled from the experiences of the companies and the managers that we interacted with while doing our research for this book. We also identify a set of steps or actions that managers can undertake to put the ideas described in this book into practice.

We start by briefly describing the context for the digital-related enterprise capabilities—the inconsistencies that can arise when a multinational pursues digital global business connectivity.

Table 10.1

Digital global business connectivity

	Intensity of localization forces			
Type of connectivity	Government regulations and policies	Business, data, and digital infrastructure	Business and consumer culture	Strategies and approaches
Company-market connectivity	Low	Low	Low to moderate	Global channel integration
	Moderate to high	Moderate to high	High	Digital first
Brand-customer connectivity	Low to moderate	Low	Low	Digital globalness
	High	Moderate to high	Moderate to high	Digital culturation
Platform-market connectivity	Low	Low	Low to moderate	Global platform
	Moderate to migh	Moderate to High	High	Regional platform
Company-ecosystem connectivity	Low	Low to moderate	Low	Digital embrace
	Moderate to high	High	Moderate to high	Digital handshake
Company-subsidiary connectivity	Low	Low	Low	Intelligent hub
	Moderate to high	Moderate to high	Moderate to high	Intelligent hub/ intelligent edge
Company-innovation source connectivity	Low	Low to moderate	Low	Digital partnership
	Moderate to high	High	Moderate to high	Digital hub
Company-innovation asset connectivity	Low	Low	Low	Global asset reconfiguration
	Moderate to high	Moderate to high	Moderate to high	Regional asset reconfiguration

Potential Inconsistencies in Digital Global Business Connectivity Strategies

Different types of inconsistencies can arise in a multinational's effort to establish digital global business connectivity. Here we identify three major types of inconsistencies: foreign market inconsistencies, regional inconsistencies, and portfolio inconsistencies.

Inconsistencies within a Foreign Market

Often, a foreign market may be globalized in certain areas and localized in others. For instance, global consumer culture may coexist with trade regulations and policies imposed by the government to restrict foreign company operations. Consider the smartphone market in India. Indian consumers are highly globalized in terms of their needs and preferences, both in the low-end and the premium categories of smartphones. However, the Indian government has for a long time maintained several FDI restrictions (e.g., at least 30 percent of production materials should be procured locally) that have hindered the operations of multinationals such as Apple. Although some of these FDI-related restrictions were eased in 2019, helping Apple and other multinationals, issues emanating from the country's conflict with China provoked other types of restrictions (aimed largely at Chinese multinationals). Thus, the Indian smartphone market still presents elements of both globalized and localized markets to foreign multinationals. Without careful consideration, such inconsistencies that exist within a foreign market may trip up a company as it adopts strategies pertaining to different dimensions of digital global business connectivity.

Inconsistencies within a Geographical Region

The extent of globalization and localization may also vary considerably within a geographical region, requiring different approaches to the markets within it, even when a single business unit of the multinational may be responsible for the entire region. For example, though the EU presents a uniform set of trade policies to foreign multinationals, the different countries within it have started to diverge considerably when it comes to certain other areas, including immigration and consumer culture. Nationalistic and protectionist tendencies are stronger in certain parts of the EU (Poland, Italy) than in others (Germany), presenting different operating environments for foreign multinationals. Thus, though a multinational may find it easier to adopt a region-wide approach to digital global business connectivity, the inconsistencies in different markets within a region likely demand more nuanced sets of strategies and practices.

Inconsistencies within a Multinational's Portfolio

Many multinationals operate in more than one industry, and the extent of globalization and localization may vary considerably across different industries within the same foreign market. For example, Asian multinationals such as Tencent, Tata Group, Alibaba, and Aditya Birla Group operate in a wide range of industries that present a diverse set of operating environments even within a country. As such, strategies employed to ensure digital global connectivity may diverge considerably across the multinational's portfolio of businesses within a foreign market. For instance, consider the Chinese smartphone companies Xiaomi, Vivo, and Oppo. Together, these companies have captured about 55 percent of the total Indian smartphone market (with Xiaomi owning about 30 percent). At the same time, both Xiaomi and Oppo also operate in the financial services market in India, primarily in online lending. However, the regulatory environments in these two markets are very different (with the Indian government tightening the FDI restrictions related to nonbanking financial services), thus requiring different strategies for digital global business connectivity. Such inconsistencies within a multinational's portfolio in a foreign market form another critical challenge.

Importantly, all of these inconsistencies are dynamic as government regulations, infrastructure, and business/consumer culture continually evolve. This in turn makes digital global business connectivity often a moving target, further intensifying the complexity of maintaining coherence across the enterprise. As we discuss next, multinationals' success in this environment is largely dependent on their digital technology–related enterprise capabilities—specifically, employee-level digital mindfulness, business unit–level digital intelligence, and organization-level digital resilience.

Digital Mindfulness and Digital Intelligence

In most of our discussions with senior executives of multinationals across the world, one theme emerged clearly—the need for all employees of a multinational to be ever vigilant and mindful of all the signals, especially the weak signals, that emanate from the international markets in which the company operates. And in a global business that is immersed in digital environments, such signals are also often digital in nature, implying the significance of a new type of capability, one we term *digital mindfulness*.

As digital technologies are infused into most workplaces across industries, it is clear that employees will need to make effective use of a diverse set of digital technologies to carry out their daily tasks, as well as to interact with others, create new knowledge, and solve problems. But in this pandemic age, when the physical office is being replaced by the virtual workplace (e.g., Siemens will let its 140,000 employees in forty-three countries work from anywhere permanently) and most business processes and interactions occur in digital environments, the ability to use different digital technologies is not likely to be sufficient.[1] Instead, employees will also need to develop the ability to eschew digital distractions and maintain continued cognitive focus on their primary tasks in order to make better-informed and holistic decisions. Research has shown that such employee mindfulness—the degree to which individuals are mindful in their work settings or maintain present-focused consciousness—can enhance work performance and contribute to employee wellness.[2]

Mindfulness involves not only being in the here and now, but also paying close attention to (and being aware of) all stimuli in an open and accepting way. In short, *mindfulness* is a state of active awareness, a propensity for continual creation and refinement, an openness to new information, and a willingness to view contexts from multiple perspectives. All of this assumes particular significance as multinationals' employees are increasingly called upon to navigate a highly digitized business environment that is susceptible to dynamic global and local forces.

Thus, here we draw on this notion of mindfulness and define *digital mindfulness* as maintaining present-focused consciousness of one's digital interactions and activities in the workplace and being open to all stimuli in an open and nonjudgmental way (see table 10.2). Such digital mindfulness allows a person not only to be fully engaged in current tasks and activities and to better manage digital distractions but also to promote divergent thinking and creativity. It also allows employees to use their diverse skills and capabilities (cognitive, social, and emotional) related to the use of digital technologies in such a way as to successfully navigate the dynamic digital global business landscape,

Table 10.2

Enterprise capabilities and digital global business connectivity

Concept	Focus	Description
Digital mindfulness	Employee	Maintaining present-focused consciousness of one's digital interactions and activities in the workplace and being open to all stimuli in an open and nonjudgmental way
Digital intelligence (*builds on digital mindfulness*)	Team or business unit	Capabilities that enable individual teams and business units to nurture and maintain the quality of a multinational's digitally enabled global business connectivity fabric
Digital resilience (*builds on digital mindfulness and digital intelligence*)	Organization	Digitization-enabled distinctive capabilities to anticipate, withstand, and rapidly adapt to or recover from adverse events that significantly impede a multinational's core businesses and performance across the world

in terms of both challenges and opportunities and in pursuit of company goals.

Digital mindfulness thus has an attentional component (being focused on the here and the now) and an attitudinal component (having open-minded curiosity)—both of which are critical in the context of maintaining a multinational's digital global business connectivity.[3] Being attentive and focused makes employees aware of and allows them to comprehend better the nature and dynamics of digital and local forces at play in their particular global business environment. At the same time, willingness to evaluate such information with an open mind and from multiple perspectives enables them to be more innovative or creative in coming up with ideas to address connectivity-related challenges. Digital technologies and platforms—in particular, social media, AI, and other data analytics techniques—now help generate a number of market-related signals and insights. But as Unilever's Stan Sthanunathan noted, "If individual managers, especially those working in subsidiaries, are not mindful of these weak yet important signals, there is not much else the company can do."[4] Indeed, despite all the fancy AI-based technologies, the first line of defense (and offense) for any multinational against the onslaught of rapid changes in a foreign market context is its employees' digital mindfulness.

Multinationals need to invest in and nurture their employees' digital mindfulness. In recent years, evidence has accumulated on how tailored programs and techniques can help cultivate mindfulness skills among employees. Many multinationals, including SAP, Goldman Sachs, Intel, Salesforce, Bosch, Target, and General Mills, have introduced mindfulness training programs and interventions to help their employees develop critical skills related to maintaining focus and coping with work-related stress and distractions.[5] Perhaps one of the better-known programs in this vein is the Search Inside Yourself program pioneered by Google in 2007. The concept of digital mindfulness introduced here emphasizes digital work environments as the primary context for nurturing and practicing such acquired mindfulness skills.

To ensure digital global business connectivity, multinationals will need to go beyond such individual-level digital mindfulness and also cultivate a higher-order competence, *digital intelligence*, which operates at team and business unit levels.[6] In much of this book, we discussed how digital technologies have become the most important or critical part of the international business fabric that connects a multinational with its global customers, ecosystems, operations, and resources. We view *digital intelligence* as the monitoring, evaluation, decision-making, and execution capabilities that enable teams and business units to nurture and maintain the quality of a multinational's digitally enabled global business connectivity fabric.

Digital intelligence thus constitutes capabilities that reside at team/ business unit levels to continuously monitor and evaluate the dynamic business landscape in a foreign market; to consider new digital technologies in conjunction with the missing links in the multinational's connectivity with customers, partners, and resources in the foreign market; and to reconfigure/reorient a subsidiary's digital connectivity with different parts of the business in that market. In other words, it reflects the ability to contextualize the knowledge about the value of one or more digital technologies vis-à-vis a multinational's business in a foreign market and to pursue actions that align such value with the subsidiary's changing goals and priorities in that market. And to the extent that it calls for individual employees in a business unit or subsidiary to be attentive to the dynamics of their immediate foreign business context and open to diverse interpretations and alternate solutions, such digital intelligence builds on employee-level digital mindfulness.

Although training and skill development in the use of digital technologies forms an important avenue to build digital intelligence, propagating the right digital culture in the enterprise is equally important. This can be accomplished in different ways. For example, Johnson Controls recently established a new top leadership position that merged the roles of the chief digital officer (CDO) and the chief customer officer (CCO), a very explicit signal to all stakeholders (including its employees) of the central role that digital technologies play in creating value for customers in an intelligent building management company. As Mike Ellis, who holds this leadership position, noted, it has helped the company make sure that technology deployment is not viewed "as a silo around digital technology, but rather as the infusion of great technology that is the cornerstone of the businesses that make up Johnson Controls."[7]

Similarly, Unilever enrolled its senior managers leaders in a reverse-mentoring program, in which some of the younger digital-native employees acted as mentors to these senior leaders. The company found that such an initiative can act as a digital cultural intervention across the enterprise, sowing the seeds of a culture that emphasizes cross-functional integrative learning on the use of digital technologies and the value of being open to experimenting with new ideas around the application of digital technologies. Importantly, such initiatives can also drive conversations around the dimensions (or elements) of digital global business connectivity that assume particular significance in the context of a multinational and help focus the attention of both individual employees and business units.

In addition, sharing of experiential knowledge gained from establishing or redesigning digital global connectivity in different subsidiaries could also contribute to building digital connectivity intelligence. Recall Philip Morris International's ongoing efforts to build intelligence in regional hubs and frontline units (intelligent edges). The company recently discovered a consistent pattern in some of the inconsistencies that arose related to the integration of data and digital connectivity across the company's product/supply chain networks. A careful analysis showed that the inconsistencies arose from lack of standardization of output metrics across its different global partners. The rapid sharing of such learnings across the enterprise can be critical in enhancing the digital intelligence of frontline business units.

As we discuss next, digital intelligence thus nurtured can contribute to a broader organizational-level capability: digital resilience, which is needed to respond to drastic external disruptions.

Digital Resilience and Digital Global Business Connectivity

Resilience is a term that has been thrown about considerably in the popular business media in recent years and months, particularly in the midst of the COVID-19 pandemic.[8] The common understanding of the term is the capacity to recover or bounce back from adversity or challenging times. Business scholars have long studied organizational resilience, although there is a lack of consensus on what it means and how it can be achieved.[9]

Here we consider resilience as an organizational capability to respond to adverse or disruptive events—importantly, not only to past events (adaptation), but also to current or ongoing events (coping) and future events (anticipation).[10] In other words, resilient organizations should be not only reactive and able to adapt to a crisis once it has occurred but also able to cope with a crisis as it is unfolding and to anticipate or sense potential adversities even before they occur. *Anticipation* involves capabilities related to sensing/detecting adversities and developing action plans or preparing for them; *coping* involves capabilities related to rapid sensemaking (giving meaning to collective experiences) of an ongoing problem or crisis and coming up with innovative solutions; and *adaptation* involves capabilities related to learning or developing a deeper understanding of some adverse event that has occurred and making changes in the organization to adapt to the new normal (or for the long term). Thus, underlying resilience are some very basic capabilities: environmental scanning and sensing, planning, sensemaking, creativity, learning, and change management.

In the context of this book, *adverse events* relate to rapid and unexpected changes in the globalization/localization forces in a foreign market and the inconsistencies that they trigger in a multinational's digital global business connectivity strategies and practices. Thus, the more dynamic the localization forces are in a foreign market, the greater the organizational resilience that is called for.

As we have seen so far, in contemporary global businesses, digital technologies increasingly form the very means and basis for value creation; as such, the capabilities associated with organizational resilience are also increasingly embedded in the same digital technologies. Thus, here we prefer to use the term *digital resilience* to denote the fact that the foundation for such resilience lies in digital technology–enabled capabilities. Note that in popular business media, digital resilience has been defined in very narrow terms to mean the ability to recover from cyberattacks or cybercrime.[11]

Here, we adopt a broader organizational capability perspective and define *digital resilience* as a multinational's digitization-enabled distinctive capabilities to anticipate, withstand, and rapidly adapt to or recover from adverse events or hardships that significantly impede its core businesses and performance across the world.

Several illustrations of such digital resilience are available from the recent COVID-19 crisis. Most companies across the world were able to cope with the COVID-19 crisis by enabling their employees to work from home using appropriate digital and data security infrastructures. Consider Wipro, an Indian multinational that offers digital technology and business process solutions to clients (mostly large multinationals) across the world. Typically, its employees are colocated at client sites in different parts of the world to ensure not only that they are able to interact closely with client managers but that they are also able to work with highly confidential client business data. When the pandemic crisis unfolded, all of this became unfeasible, but the work could not stop. The company responded by rapidly (over about two weeks) putting together a highly secure and reliable digital infrastructure that its employees sitting in their homes could connect with in order to continue their work for foreign clients. Although some client companies were apprehensive at the start, they soon gained enough confidence in Wipro's digital infrastructure and capabilities to maintain both the needed interaction intensity and data security. Indeed, Wipro's experience during this crisis has made the company question the value of colocating employees in client sites and rethink its approach to client servicing.

Similarly, many multinationals, including Johnson & Johnson, were able to adapt to the crisis by using digital simulation tools to quickly redesign their global supply chains and find alternate paths to get foreign suppliers to supply manufacturing plants in different parts of the world. In short, diverse types of digital technology–based capabilities allowed companies to not only cope with the crisis as it unfolded but also adapt to its long-term impact on their global operations.

Digital intelligence and digital mindfulness form a critical source of such resilience. Specifically, digital intelligence provides digitally enabled capabilities to both sense and respond to adversities and thereby helps build digital resilience. For instance, employees' digital mindfulness can help multinationals detect weak signals related to an approaching disruptive force, and digital intelligence capabilities enable it to evaluate such weak signals in conjunction with information acquired from other sources. Similarly, digital intelligence capabilities enable a multinational to identify where, when, and what resources should be best deployed or to do so in the most productive way, thus helping the firm to cultivate, maneuver, and improvise existing resources and capabilities to cope with or adapt to adverse events. Further, digital intelligence also helps establish cross-border, interunit collaboration initiatives—curtailing structural inertia and bureaucratic hurdles—when faced with rapidly evolving operational disruptions. Such digital intelligence can also enhance a multinational's ability to connect with diverse external stakeholders in a foreign market, thereby sensitizing the organization to local conditions and in turn allowing the company to anticipate adverse events more effectively.

Other types of organizational-level capabilities also contribute to digital resilience, including the company's entrepreneurial orientation, collaboration capabilities, and learning and experimentation cultures. Increasingly, many such capabilities are also facilitated by digital technologies. For example, in earlier chapters, we discussed how digital simulation tools and digital experimentation platforms allow multinationals to evaluate different aspects of their digital global business connectivity.

Digital mindfulness, digital intelligence, and digital resilience not only complement one another (see table 10.2) but also collectively enable a multinational to successfully navigate the increasingly complex and dynamic set of localization forces that prevail in different parts of the world. These capabilities are essential for a multinational to establish its digital global business connectivity and, importantly, to maintain its continued relevance. Indeed, without sufficient investment in building these capabilities, a multinational will lose its sensitivity to potentially disruptive events in foreign markets and the ability to address the strategic inconsistences that they provoke.

Core Themes and Perspectives

As part of our research for this book, over the past few years, we talked with senior and mid-level managers in a number of multinationals across different industries and in different geographical regions. Their diverse perspectives and experiences have richly informed many of the ideas and concepts described so far in this book. At the same time, there are a few themes that were consistently emphasized in all of our interactions with managers. These themes are indeed reflected in our discussions in this book. However, we believe they are worth highlighting here once again as they go beyond individual strategies and practices and reflect a broader set of insights and approaches related to digital global business connectivity that underpins our book.

The Duality of Digital in Global Business

As we noted at the beginning of this book, globalization forces are not going to go away anytime soon, but neither are deglobalization (localization) forces. Digitization can and should be viewed by business managers as a vehicle to successfully navigate these two alternate global business contexts. As the numerous examples and cases described in this book illustrate, digital technologies help companies to rapidly scale their operations in other countries, transfer and deploy their assets across borders, and coordinate and optimize global operations and resource usage—all of which builds on the globalization forces at play. The very same digital technologies, however, also help infuse considerable strategic and operational flexibility and looseness into a multinational's global business, allowing it to evolve and adapt its strategies in step with changes in the localization forces in specific countries or regions.

It is this *duality of digital* that was emphasized by all the business managers that we interacted with over the past few years. It was clear to us that managers who understand this consider both globalization and localization forces as opportunities to expand their global business by exercising their company's digital muscles, albeit in different ways. As one senior manager noted, most multinationals are attuned to the traditional view of digitizing as a way to enhance efficiency and discipline in global expansion and operations, but few can simultaneously hold the alternate view of digitizing as a means of loosening their control and infusing more options.

Multinationals that are successful in the future will be those that can incorporate this duality of digital into all of their global business thinking in a fundamental way. And we hope that the practical ideas and steps outlined in this book will help them move in that direction.

Digital Global Business Connectivity Is a Business Capability

When we first introduced the concept of digital global business connectivity (in chapter 2), we noted that it is a business capability, not a technological or digital capability. We hope the discussion since then has helped to reinforce this idea in your mind, but perhaps it is important to highlight it once more.

As several of the managers we talked with indicated, the term *digital* often tends to skew the discussion (and the attention of managers) away from the business goal or purpose and toward the realm of new and fanciful technologies, be they IoT, 5G, or virtualization, and their purported capabilities. Admittedly, by appending the term *digital* to *global business connectivity*, we took a risk here in that your attention may focus more on the digital part of the discussion, leading you to interpret this as a digital capability. But nothing is farther from the truth.

The end goal is to enable a multinational to connect with all aspects of its global business—from customers and partners to resources and operations—in both globalized and localized environments. And digital technology is needed there only to serve this purpose.

Thus, the first question in a business manager's mind should always relate to the implications of globalization and localization forces on a multinational's connectivity or relationships with various elements of its global business. Only after that first question is answered should the second question, how digital technologies can help multinationals address the associated challenges, come up. And if you recall, that is how we listed the central questions in each of the chapters.

Such an approach, which privileges the business capabilities over the digital capabilities, will allow multinationals and their managers to anchor their attention on the strategies and practices that underlie and power digital global business connectivity.

The Need to Focus on Middle Ground Strategies

A key insight from our research for this book was the need for multinationals to carefully decide on the extent of coupling with key elements of their global business based on the nature and type of localization forces present in an international market context. We introduced the notion of tight and loose coupling as a foundation for such thinking. And in discussing this in the various chapters, we identified the prototypical strategies that reflect both tight coupling and loose coupling.

But often, the globalization and localization forces operate simultaneously in a particular international market. As Bijoy Sagar of Bayer AG noted, "sometimes the signals coming from a [foreign] market are mixed . . . some seem to invite us there while some deter us."[12] For example, when government policies are dictated by day-to-day political issues, they may end up being not quite coherent, opening up the economy in some respects while closing it in other ways. Similarly, as we have seen in the case of several EU member countries, a globalized consumer culture may coexist with and run counter to a more protectionist set of trade policies adopted by the government. All of these highlight the need for companies to carefully calibrate the desired extent of tightness or looseness and adopt middle ground strategies that best fit into a foreign market context.

In this book, we have provided several avenues for companies to adopt such an approach. For example, they could adopt tighter coupling with regard to customers and markets while focusing on looser coupling with regard to operations and activities. In other words, tight coupling on one dimension of digital global business connectivity may be combined with loose coupling on another. Further, even within a dimension—say, connectivity with customers—companies can consider different design elements, from the use of global or local influencers to the use of global or regional digital platforms and infrastructures, in order to deploy strategies that represent different flavors of tightness and looseness in their relationships.

The bottom line is that companies should treat the prototypical strategies prescribed in this book as guideposts and be creative in coming up with strategies for digital global business connectivity that best serve a particular foreign market context.

Global Business Leadership in the New Normal Digital World

As we laid out earlier, digitization of global business has brought forth the need for new types of capabilities, at all levels of a multinational, that relate to how the company detects or acquires weak and strong signals in an international business context, analyzes that information, and incorporates it into decision-making—and, more broadly, to how the company maintains the overall coherence of its digital global business connectivity in times of change.

All of these capabilities reflect two broader shifts occurring in the nature of global business leadership.

First, as we have seen throughout this book, the age of "command and control" as the dominant global management approach is over. Multinationals and their senior executives need to be adept at orchestrating and influencing a diverse set of global partners, subsidiaries, markets, and resources, often loosely coupled to the company, in order to create and deliver value in international markets. CEOs and senior executives who can devise and communicate an inclusive vision for value creation in ways that allow for greater degrees of freedom in how such a vision is enacted or realized in different international markets and geographical regions are likely to be more successful. Indeed, a premium will be placed on CEOs (and other senior executives) who are comfortable operating in a business world that emits mixed signals related to globalization and deglobalization and are able to match that with the right balance of tightness and looseness in their company's relationships.

Second, if there is one thing evident from our discussions so far in this book, it is that digital will be a critical part of the solution in addressing the challenge we just discussed. As such, digital should not be an area of decision-making that is left just for the company's chief information officer (CIO) or CDO. Instead, digital should be everybody's business at the senior executive level, and it will be the CEO's job to ensure that the right digital culture pervades the entire organization, including, most importantly, the C-suite.

Think about human resources. All companies have a chief human resource officer or a chief people officer. But that doesn't mean that CEOs don't focus on people management skills. Indeed, a CEO without superior people skills is unlikely to be successful in any contemporary organization. It is the same with digital. Companies with CEOs (and senior executives) who have superior digital skills—who can envision and lead their organizations as *digital* organizations—will likely find greater success in this increasingly digital world we live in.

Thus, across industries, global business leadership will be defined by the ability to lead loosely coupled, digital organizations that can adapt to and thrive under the influence of both globalization and localization forces.

Next Steps—or, Actions for Monday Morning

We conclude this book with a set of recommendations on how to proceed in establishing digital global business connectivity for your company. Specifically, we have formulated a set of questions to get you started on your journey to implement the ideas and concepts advanced in this book.

Is digital global business connectivity relevant to my company? It is worthwhile to start with this important question. Pick either the foreign market that is most critical to your company or the one that presents the most challenges. Use the scales we offered in chapter 2 (tables 2.1 and 2.2) to measure the intensity of digital and regional/ local forces in that market and map it on the digital forces and regional or local forces landscape (figure 2.1). If the market falls in either quadrant C (digital globalization) or quadrant D (digital localization), digital global business connectivity is very relevant, and potentially quite important for your company's continued success in that market.

What aspect of digital global business connectivity should I start with? While most multinationals would find all four dimensions of digital global business connectivity—customers and markets, partners and ecosystems, activities and operations, and resources and knowledge— equally important, it would be advisable to start with a focus on one of those. Pick the dimension that is most crucial to your success in the pertinent foreign market or pick the dimension that is likely to be most impacted by localization forces. Then focus on the relevant elements of digital global business connectivity (table 10.1) and consider the strategies that would be appropriate.

As we discussed a short while back, the strategies described in this book are meant to be prototypical; you should treat them as starting points for discussions with your team. Bring together all the information that you have acquired so far related to the selected dimension in the foreign market and get the creative juices flowing. Each company will need to come up with unique strategies that fit with its particular set of challenges and market context.

Do I have the requisite capabilities to undertake this initiative? This is a good question to ask early on by itself. Our research has shown that most multinationals do not ask it—at least, not yet. In this chapter, we described some of the capabilities—at employee, team/business unit, and organizational levels—that are critical for making the digital global business connectivity strategies work. If you are convinced that digital global business connectivity is relevant to your company, then identifying and investing in these digital capabilities should be one of your first steps. You probably are not starting from scratch; many such capabilities may already exist, but perhaps not all and perhaps not in every part of your company. Develop a plan to build digital intelligence and digital resilience. That certainly is not something that can be achieved overnight, but it is important to take the first step today.

How do I scale this initiative? We are firm believers in the idea of starting small, testing ideas, and then pursuing scaled implementation. Thus we suggested that you start by identifying one foreign market and one dimension of digital global business connectivity. But digital global business connectivity is an enterprise-wide phenomenon, and to get the full gains you have to scale up to include all four dimensions and all the major international markets your company operates in. We suggest that you expand your efforts to incorporate other foreign markets in a measured way, calibrating your efforts based on the investments you can afford to make and the returns you experience.

We are confident that the returns from the time and effort your company invests in pursuing digital global business connectivity will be evident in both the short term and the long term. Indeed, as we noted at the beginning of this book (as well as at the start of this chapter), digitization and localization forces have together created a new normal for global businesses, and digital global business connectivity is increasingly not an option but a prerequisite for success in this new world.

Good luck on your journey to establish digital global business connectivity in your company and to transform it into a digital multinational!

Acknowledgments

This book had its genesis in a long and interesting conversation that the two of us, Satish and Yadong, had at one of the recent Annual Academy of Management meetings. We discovered that both of us were fascinated by the emergent complex international business landscape shaped by globalization and deglobalization forces and the role that digital technologies could potentially play in helping companies navigate it.

Researching about this phenomenon and writing this book has been a labor of love and joy for both of us, but one in which we found generous encouragement and valuable support from many people, both in academia and in the industry, to whom we acknowledge our deep gratitude. In particular, we benefited tremendously from our conversations with the following people, each of whom generously gave their time and shared their valuable insights on a wide range of related topics: Zaved Akhtar, B. P. Biddappa (aka Dinesh), Harish Bijoor, Jurgen Brock, Mike Fisher, Nitin Manoharan, D. Narain, Bijoy Sagar, Shiv Shivakumar, Stan Sthanunathan, Harit Talwar, Deep Thomas, Himanshu Wardhan, and Jeroen Wels. Satish would like to extend his special thanks to Dinesh (his former classmate) and Stan for going beyond the call of duty and connecting him with a number of their colleagues at Unilever. In addition, there are many others who critiqued our early ideas and helped sharpen our thinking and to whom we are much indebted.

We would like to thank Conny Braams, the chief digital and marketing officer at Unilever, for making the time in her hectic schedule to write the foreword for our book. Her experience in the past year or so as Unilever's CDMO, in building a future-fit digital multinational, reflects and underlines much of our own thinking on this topic. As such, we are indeed grateful to Conny for her support of the ideas expounded upon in this book.

In the realm of academia, we would like to acknowledge our profound gratitude to our dear friend and colleague Shaker Zahra, who introduced us to each other about five years back and also worked with us on a research paper. We also acknowledge the valuable comments and suggestions we received from three anonymous reviewers on the initial draft of this book.

Satish would like to express his deep gratitude to Joe Keithley, who not only endowed the chair that he holds at Case Western Reserve University but also championed his work in different ways. Joe has been a trusted friend right from the time Satish joined Case. He values his numerous conversations with Joe over the years and is also grateful for his frequent visits to Satish's class on new product development.

Satish also thanks, Kalle Lyytinen, his friend, colleague, and department chair at Case, who may have inadvertently initiated this book project by asking, "So when are you going to write your next book?" not long after Satish had joined Case. Kalle has been a wonderful coauthor in his other research projects, particularly in the area of digital innovation.

We would like to thank Paul Michelman, editor in chief of *MIT Sloan Management Review*, and Emily Taber, our editor at the MIT Press, for believing enough in our early ideas for this book to get us started on the path to writing it. Emily has truly been a great partner for us in this project. She patiently read and gave us invaluable input on the numerous drafts that we submitted to her, ever careful to retain our thinking and perspectives while helping us to sharpen them further. We would also like to thank Kathleen Caruso and the rest of the MIT Press team for their commitment and enthusiastic support. A special thanks to our exceptional copy editor Melinda Rankin for her thorough and careful work in enhancing the clarity of our writing. Acknowledgments are also due to Elizabeth Heichler of *MIT Sloan Management Review* for her support and encouragement of our ideas.

Last, both of us would like to acknowledge our gratitude to our families for their support while we were researching and writing this book. Satish would like to express his deep gratitude to his wife Priya for her constant encouragement and unending support throughout the writing of this book. He is also grateful to his eleven-year-old twin sons, Ashok and Bharat, for the immense joy and playfulness they bring to his life. This book is dedicated to them.

Notes

Chapter 1

1. See V. Hansen, *The Year 1000: When Explorers Connected the World and Globalization Began* (New York: Scribner, 2020). It should be noted that trade links have existed even in prehistoric periods—for example, between the Sumer and the Indus Valley Civilization in the third millennium BC. And even after that, around first-century BC, luxury goods (such as silk) and spices were traded between Asia and Europe via the Silk Road and other trade routes. However, it was not until the territorial expansionary moves reached all five continents that truly global trade routes were established and maintained.

2. P. Vanham, *A Brief History of Globalization*, World Economic Forum Report, January 17, 2019, https://www.weforum.org/agenda/2019/01/how-globalization-4-0-fits-into-the-history-of-globalization/.

3. M. Jaworek and M. Kuzel, "Transnational Corporations in the World Economy: Formation, Development and Present Position," *Copernican Journal of Finance & Accounting* 4, no. 1 (2015): 55–70.

4. *Multinational Enterprises in the Global Economy*, OECD Report, May 2018, https://www.oecd.org/industry/ind/MNEs-in-the-global-economy-policy-note.pdf.

5. "India's Smartphone Market Grows by a Modest 8% YoY in 2019 Shipping 152.5 Million Units, IDC India Reports," IDC, February 7, 2020, https://www.idc.com/getdoc.jsp?containerId=prAP46013620.

6. Based on a talk given by Jeroen Tas, the Chief Innovation and Strategy Officer at Royal Phillips, at S. Nambisan's EMBA class in spring 2019.

7. P. A. Van Bergeijk, *Deglobalization 2.0: Trade and Openness during the Great Depression and the Great Recession* (Cheltenham, UK: Edward Elgar Publishing, 2019).

8. A. Tappe, "The Economy as We Knew It Might Be Over, Fed Chairman Says," CNN, November 12, 2020, https://www.cnn.com/2020/11/12/economy/economy-after-covid-powell/index.html.

9. T. A. Madiega, *Digital Sovereignty for Europe*, European Parliament Briefing Paper, July 2020, https://www.europarl.europa.eu/RegData/etudes/BRIE/2020/651992/EPRS_BRI(2020)651992_EN.pdf.

10. "DHL Global Connectedness Index: Globalization Hits New Record High," DHL, press release, February 12, 2019, https://www.dpdhl.com/en/media-relations/press-releases/2019/dhl-global-connectedness-index-2018.html.

11. A. Baig, B. Hall, P. Jenkins, E. Lamarre, and B. McCarthy, "The COVID-19 Recovery Will Be Digital: A Plan for the First 90 Days," McKinsey & Company, May 14, 2020, https://www.mckinsey.com/business-functions/mckinsey-digital/our-insights/the-COVID-19-recovery-will-be-digital-a-plan-for-the-first-90-days.

12. "Reflections on Investing During a Crisis," Shaw Spring Partners, May 15, 2020, https://www.jaguaranalytics.com/wp-content/uploads/2020/05/ShawString-Quarterly-Letter.pdf.

13. "Six Months That Will Change Global Food Security, One Way or the Other," Bayer CropScience, accessed March 19, 2021, https://www.cropscience.bayer.com/people-planet/global-impact/a/smallholders-coronavirus-and-food-security.

14. T. L. Friedman, "Our New Historical Divide: B.C. and A.C.—the World before Corona and the World After," *New York Times*, March 17, 2020, https://www.nytimes.com/2020/03/17/opinion/coronavirus-trends.html.

15. United Nations Conference on Trade and Development, *World Investment Report 2020* (Geneva: United Nations, 2020), https://unctad.org/system/files/official-document/wir2020_overview_en.pdf.

16. "Has Covid-19 Killed Globalisation?," *Economist*, May 16, 2020, https://www.economist.com/leaders/2020/05/14/has-covid-19-killed-globalisation.

17. J. Manyika, S. Lund, J. Bughin, J. R. Woetzel, K. Stamenov, and D. Dhingra, *Digital Globalization: The New Era of Global Flows* (San Francisco, CA: McKinsey Global Institute, February 24, 2016), https://www.mckinsey.com/business

-functions/mckinsey-digital/our-insights/digital-globalization-the-new-era-of -global-flows.

18. "Digital in 2020," We Are Social, accessed March 19, 2021], https:// wearesocial.com/digital-2020.

19. R. Dobbs, J. Manyika, and J. Woetzel, "The Four Global Forces Breaking All the Trends," McKinsey Global Institute, April 1, 2015, https://www.mckinsey .com/business-functions/strategy-and-corporate-finance/our-insights/the-four -global-forces-breaking-all-the-trends#.

20. T. L. Friedman, "After the Pandemic, a Revolution in Education and Work Awaits," *New York Times*, October 20, 2020, https://www.nytimes.com/2020 /10/20/opinion/covid-education-work.html.

21. V. Govindarajan and R. Ramamurti, "Reverse Innovation, Emerging Markets, and Global Strategy," *Global Strategy Journal* 1, no. 3–4 (2011): 191–205; V. Govindarajan and C. Trimble, *Reverse Innovation: Create Far from Home, Win Everywhere* (Brighton, MA: Harvard Business Review Press, 2012).

22. Interview with S. Nambisan on October 14, 2020.

23. Hansen, *The Year 1000*.

24. M. Mueller, *Will the Internet Fragment? Sovereignty, Globalization and Cyberspace* (Cambridge: Polity Press, 2017).

25. A. Segal, *China's Vision for Cyber Sovereignty and the Global Governance of Cyberspace*, National Bureau of Asian Research Special Report #87, https:// www.nbr.org/publication/chinas-vision-for-cyber-sovereignty-and-the-global -governance-of-cyberspace/.

26. "Coronavirus Impact on Retail E-commerce Website Traffic Worldwide as of June 2020, by Average Monthly Visits," Statista, July 2020, https://www.statista .com/statistics/1112595/covid-19-impact-retail-e-commerce-site-traffic-global/.

27. Prior research in the area of international business has conceptualized connectivity primarily in terms of pipelines of information (knowledge) flows for innovation—either among MNEs or among individuals and MNEs. See U. Andersson, Á. Dasí, R. Mudambi, and T. Pedersen, "Technology, Innovation and Knowledge: The Importance of Ideas and International Connectivity," *Journal of World Business* 51, no. 1 (2016): 153–162; M. Cano-Kollmann, J. Cantwell, T. J. Hannigan, R. Mudambi, and J. Song, "Knowledge Connectivity: An Agenda for Innovation Research in International Business," *Journal of*

International Business Studies 47, no. 2 (2016): 255–262; E. Turkina and A. Van Assche, "Global Connectedness and Local Innovation in Industrial Clusters," *Journal of International Business Studies* 49, no. 6 (2018): 706–728.

28. In the summer of 2020, we conducted a questionnaire-based survey of 163 multinationals (37 percent were headquartered in the US, 12 percent in Europe, 22 percent in China, 23 percent in India and East Asia, and 6 percent in other regions). The survey respondents were senior executives in the multinationals.

29. Our notion of tight and loose coupling is derived from the *loose coupling theory*. See J. D. Orton and K. E. Weick, "Loosely Coupled Systems: A Reconceptualization," *Academy of Management Review* 15, no. 2 (1990): 203–223; K. E. Weick, *Making Sense of the Organization* (Malden, MA: Blackwell Publishing, 2001); K. E. Weick, "Educational Organizations as Loosely Coupled Systems," *Administrative Science Quarterly* 21 (1976): 1–19.

Chapter 2

1. H. Kotani and J. Suzuki, "Southeast Asia Seeks Ways to Protect Car Industry," Nikkei Asia, October 23, 2018, https://asia.nikkei.com/Business/Business -trends/Southeast-Asia-seeks-ways-to-protect-car-industry.

2. "The Growth in Connected IoT Devices is Expected to Generate 79.4ZB of Data in 2025, According to a New IDC Forecast," Business Wire, June 18, 2019, https://www.businesswire.com/news/home/20190618005012/en/The-Growth -in-Connected-IoT-Devices-is-Expected-to-Generate-79.4ZB-of-Data-in-2025 -According-to-a-New-IDC-Forecast.

3. For more on this and other digital technology characteristics, see J. Kallinikos, A. Aaltonen, and A. Marton, "The Ambivalent Ontology of Digital Artifacts," *MIS Quarterly* 37, no. 2 (2013): 357–370.

4. For more on the concept of generativity in the context of digital technologies, see J. Zittrain, "The Generative Internet," *Harvard Law Review* 119, no. 7 (2006): 1975–2040; Y. Yoo, O. Henfridsson, and K. Lyytinen, "The New Organizing Logic of Digital Innovation: An Agenda for Information Systems Research," *Information Systems Research* 21, no. 4 (2010): 724–735.

5. For example, see the following reports: W. Sarni, C. White, R. Webb, K. Cross, and R. Glotzbach, *Digital Water* (London: IWA, June 2019), https://iwa -network.org/wp-content/uploads/2019/06/IWA_2019_Digital_Water_Report .pdf; A. Gosine, "Big Value for Big Data in Water," *WaterWorld*, May 2, 2019,

https://www.waterworld.com/technologies/amr-ami/article/16227142/big
-value-for-big-data-in-water.

6. *Connected Car Market by Service*, Research and Markets, report 5135731, July
2020, https://www.researchandmarkets.com/reports/4863432/.

7. Interview with S. Nambisan in April 2020.

8. *Cisco Annual Internet Report (2018–2023)*, Cisco, March 9, 2020, https://www
.cisco.com/c/en/us/solutions/collateral/executive-perspectives/annual-internet
-report/white-paper-c11-741490.html; *VNI Complete Forecast Highlights*, Cisco,
accessed March 19, 2021, https://www.cisco.com/c/dam/m/en_us/solutions
/service-provider/vni-forecast-highlights/pdf/India_Device_Growth_Traffic
_Profiles.pdf.

9. *DHL Global Connectedness Index 2020*, DHL, accessed March 19, 2021, https://
www.dhl.com/global-en/home/insights-and-innovation/thought-leadership/
case-studies/global-connectedness-index.html.

10. A. Faiola, "The Virus That Shut Down the World," *Seattle Times*, June 27, 2020,
https://www.seattletimes.com/nation-world/the-virus-that-shut-down-the-world/.

11. "Regional Trade Agreements," World Trade Organization, accessed March
22, 2021, https://www.wto.org/english/tratop_e/region_e/region_e.htm#facts.

12. "Digital Walls on the Rise," Kearney, accessed March 22, 2021, https://
www.kearney.com/web/global-business-policy-council/article?/a/digital-walls
-on-the-rise; R. Zhong and K. Shultz, "With India's TikTok Ban, the World's Digital Walls Grow Higher," *New York Times*, July 11, 2020, https://www.nytimes
.com/2020/06/30/technology/india-china-tiktok.html.

13. Interview with S. Nambisan in May 2020.

14. For example, see Y. Liu, W. Tao, and W. H. S. Tsai, "Global versus Local
Consumer Culture Positioning in a Transitional Market: Understanding the
Influence of Consumer Nationalism," *International Journal of Strategic Communi-
cation* 11, no. 4 (2017): 344–360.

15. J. Y. Cheng and B. Groysberg, "How Corporate Cultures Differ around the
World," *Harvard Business Review*, January 8, 2020, https://hbr.org/2020/01/how
-corporate-cultures-differ-around-the-world.

16. S. Rajan, J. Bhattacharya, Y. Mandviwalla, and D. Jain, "Changing Gears
2020: How Digital Is Transforming the Face of the Automotive Industry," Bain &
Company, May 9, 2017, https://www.bain.com/insights/changing-gears-2020/.

17. For more on this, see J. D. Orton and K. E. Weick, "Loosely Coupled Systems: A Reconceptualization," *Academy of Management Review* 15, no. 2 (1990): 203–223.

18. Interview with S. Nambisan in May 2020.

Chapter 3

1. For example, see J. A. Quelch and E. J. Hoff, "Customizing Global Strategies. *Harvard Business Review* 64 (1986): 59–68. See also J. N. Sheth, "Impact of Emerging Markets on Marketing: Rethinking Existing Perspectives and Practices," *Journal of Marketing* 75, no. 4 (2011): 166–182.

2. F. Hovivian, "Globalization: Apple's One-Size Fits-All Approach," *Brand Quarterly*, December 19, 2016, http://www.brandquarterly.com/globalization-apples -one-size-fits-approach.

3. While the Indian government relaxed some of these restrictions in 2019, the broader set of regulations still holds.

4. *Global* (local) *consumer culture* has been defined as a social arrangement in which the relations between lived culture and social resources, and between meaningful ways of life and the symbolic and material resources on which they depend, are globally (locally) conceived and are mediated through deterritorialized, global (geographically anchored, local) markets. For more on this, see J. B. E. Steenkamp, "Global versus Local Consumer Culture: Theory, Measurement, and Future Research Directions," *Journal of International Marketing* 27, no. 1 (2019): 1–19. Tomlinson calls "localism" and "globalism" the "two axial principles of our age." J. Tomlinson, *Globalization and Culture* (Chicago: University of Chicago Press, 1999), 190.

5. A. Singhi, N. Jain, and K. Sanghi, "The New Indian: The Many Facets of a Changing Consumer," BCG, March 20, 2017, https://www.bcg.com/en-us /publications/2017/marketing-sales-globalization-new-indian-changing-consumer.

6. Interview conducted by S. Nambisan in July 2020.

7. A. Lipsman, "Global Ecommerce 2019: Ecommerce Continues Strong Gains amid Global Economic Uncertainty," Insider Intelligence, June 27, 2019, https:// www.emarketer.com/content/global-ecommerce-2019.

8. "India: Retail Ecommerce Revenue Forecast from 2017 to 2024," Statista, June 8, 2020, https://www.statista.com/statistics/289770/e-commerce-revenue -forecast-in-india/.

9. In 2016, Dollar Shave Club was acquired by Unilever.

10. J. Singh, S. Nambisan, R. G. Bridge, and J. K. U. Brock, "One-Voice Strategy for Customer Engagement," *Journal of Service Research* 24, no. 1 (2021): 42–65, https://doi.org/10.1177/1094670520910267.

11. "Lululemon Unveils Power of Three Strategic Plan to Accelerate Growth," Business Wire, April 24, 2019, https://www.businesswire.com/news/home /20190424005350/en/lululemon-Unveils-%E2%80%9CPower-of-Three%E2%80 %9D-Strategic-Plan-to-Accelerate-Growth.

12. "Walgreens and Birchbox to Offer Customers Innovative Beauty Experience In-Store and Online," Business Wire, October 4, 2018, https://www.businesswire .com/news/home/20181004005324/en/Walgreens-Birchbox-Offer-Customers -Innovative-Beauty-Experience.

13. P. Kotler, H. Kartajaya, and I. Setiawan, *Marketing 4.0: Moving from Traditional to Digital* (Hoboken, NJ: John Wiley & Sons, 2017).

14. As of 2020, the average price for 1 GB data connectivity on the Jio network is nine US cents. By comparison, the corresponding figure for the US is eight dollars. For additional details, see C. Ang, "What Does 1GB of Mobile Data Cost in Every Country?," Visual Capitalist, July 3, 2020, https://www.visualcapitalist .com/cost-of-mobile-data-worldwide/.

15. E. Xiao, "H&M Is Erased from Chinese E-Commerce over Xinjiang Stance," *Wall Street Journal*, March 25, 2021, https://www.wsj.com/articles/h-m-is-erased -from-chinese-e-commerce-over-xinjiang-stance-11616695377.

16. For a recent analysis of the implications of hyperconnectivity for brand strategy, see V. Swaminathan, A. Sorescu, J. B. E. Steenkamp, T. C. G. O'Guinn, and B. Schmitt, "Branding in a Hyperconnected World: Refocusing Theories and Rethinking Boundaries," *Journal of Marketing* 84, no. 2 (2020): 24–46.

17. For example, see F. J. Cossío-Silva, M. Á. Revilla-Camacho, M. Vega-Vázquez, and B. Palacios-Florencio, "Value Co-creation and Customer Loyalty," *Journal of Business Research* 69, no. 5 (2016): 1621–1625.

18. K. H. Hung, S. Y. Li, and R. W. Belk, "Glocal Understandings: Female Readers' Perceptions of the New Woman in Chinese Advertising," *Journal of International Business Studies* 38, no. 6 (2007): 1034–1051.

19. Interview conducted by S. Nambisan in June 2020.

20. Interview conducted by S. Nambisan in July 2020.

21. I. M. Dinner, T. Kushwaha, and J. B. E. Steenkamp, "Psychic Distance and Performance of MNCs during Marketing Crises," *Journal of International Business Studies* 50, no. 3 (2019): 339–364.

Chapter 4

1. C. Dougherty, "Inside Yelp's Six-Year Grudge against Google," *New York Times*, July 1, 2017, https://www.nytimes.com/2017/07/01/technology/yelp-google-european-union-antitrust.html.

2. C. O'Brien, "Yelp Blames Google for Its Failed International Business," VentureBeat, March 6, 2017, https://venturebeat.com/2017/03/06/yelp-blames-google-for-its-failed-international-business/.

3. M. Abi-Habib, "India Bans Nearly 60 Chinese Apps, Including TikTok and WeChat," *New York Times*, June 29, 2020, https://www.nytimes.com/2020/06/29/world/asia/tik-tok-banned-india-china.html.

4. Interview with S. Nambisan in April 2020.

5. Interview with S. Nambisan in April 2020.

6. Interview with S. Nambisan in May 2020.

7. "India's E-commerce Market Set to Surpass US$91bn in 2023," *Business Matters*, January 23, 2020, https://www.bmmagazine.co.uk/news/indias-e-commerce-market-set-to-surpass-us91bn-in-2023.

8. Interview with S. Nambisan in April 2020.

9. R. Bhatia, "Data Science in Action: Unpacking Aditya Birla Group's AI & Digital Analytics Strategy," *Analytics India Magazine*, October 22, 2019, https://analyticsindiamag.com/data-science-in-action-unpacking-aditya-birla-groups-ai-digital-analytics-strategy/.

10. FieldView is owned by the Climate Corporation, a subsidiary of Bayer AG.

11. Interview with S. Nambisan in May 2020.

12. See https://climate.com/climate-farmrise.

13. This description of Philips's HealthSuite platform ecosystem strategy has been informed by discussions held during a visit by Jeroen Tas, chief innovation and strategy officer at Philips Healthcare, during S. Nambisan's EMBA class in spring 2019.

14. "Philips and Mackenzie Health Announce 18-Year Strategic Partnership," accessed March 28, 2021, https://www.usa.philips.com/healthcare/about /enterprise-partnerships/mackenzie-health.

15. C. Sturman, "Philips and Samsung Partner to Develop Integrated Healthcare Services," Healthcare Global, March 13, 2020, https://www.healthcare global.com/technology/philips-and-samsung-partner-develop-integrated -healthcare-services.

Chapter 5

1. For more on this, see W. C. Shih, "Is It Time to Rethink Globalized Supply Chains?," *MIT Sloan Management Review*, March 19, 2020, https://sloanreview .mit.edu/article/is-it-time-to-rethink-globalized-supply-chains/; D. Simchi-Levi, "Three Scenarios to Guide Your Global Supply Chain Recovery," *MIT Sloan Management Review*, April 13, 2020, https://sloanreview.mit.edu/article/three -scenarios-to-guide-your-global-supply-chain-recovery/.

2. See M. Reeves, L. Fæste, C. Chen, P. Carlsson-Szlezak, and K. Whitaker, "How Chinese Companies Have Responded to Coronavirus," *Harvard Business Review*, March 10, 2020, https://hbr.org/2020/03/how-chinese-companies-have -responded-to-coronavirus.

3. See H. Yu and M. Greeven, "How Autonomy Creates Resilience in the Face of Crisis," *MIT Sloan Management Review*, March 23, 2020, https://sloanreview .mit.edu/article/how-autonomy-creates-resilience-in-the-face-of-crisis/.

4. For a discussion of such integration-responsiveness (I-R) balance, see J. Birkinshaw, A. Morrison, and J. Hulland, "Structural and Competitive Determinants of a Global Integration Strategy," *Strategic Management Journal* 16 (1995): 637–655; K. Roth, D. Schweiger, and A. J. Morrison, "Global Strategy Implementation at the Business Unit Level: Operational Capabilities and Administrative Mechanisms," *Journal of International Business Studies* 22, no. 3 (1991): 369–402.

5. J. Smith, "Unilever Uses Virtual Factories to Tune Up Its Supply Chain," *Wall Street Journal*, July 15, 2019. https://www.wsj.com/articles/unilever-uses -virtual-factories-to-tune-up-its-supply-chain-11563206402.

6. Interview with S. Nambisan in July 2020.

7. M. Heller, "How Johnson & Johnson IT Is Managing a Global Crisis," *CIO Magazine*, April 22, 2020, https://www.cio.com/article/3538528/how-johnson -johnson-it-is-managing-a-global-crisis.html?.

8. S. Lund, J. Manikya, and J. Woetzel, "Risk, Resilience, and Rebalancing in Global Value Chains," McKinsey Global Institute, August 6, 2020, https://www.mckinsey.com/business-functions/operations/our-insights/risk-resilience-and-rebalancing-in-global-value-chains#.

9. M. Fleming, "How Unilever Is Using AI to 'Democratise' Upskilling and Future-Proof Its Employees," Marketing Week, June 27, 2019, https://www.marketingweek.com/how-unilever-is-using-ai-to-democratise-upskilling-and-future-proof-its-employees/.

10. Interview with S. Nambisan in May 2020.

11. Interview with S. Nambisan in June 2020.

Chapter 6

1. Govindarajan and Trimble, *Reverse Innovation*; Govindarajan and Ramamurti, "Reverse Innovation, Emerging Markets, and Global Strategy."

2. "Tommy Hilfiger Commits to 3D Design to Realize Ambitious Digitalization Journey," Business Wire, November 7, 2019, https://www.businesswire.com/news/home/20191107005718/en/Tommy-Hilfiger-Commits-3D-Design-Realize-Ambitious/.

3. V. Grewall-Carr and C. Bates, *The Three Billion: Enterprise Crowdsourcing and the Growing Fragmentation of Work* (London: Deloitte, 2016), https://www2.deloitte.com/content/dam/Deloitte/de/Documents/Innovation/us-cons-enterprise-crowdsourcing-and-growing-fragmentation-of-work%20(3).pdf.

4. *Crowdsourcing Market Report 2019–2027*, Absolute Market Insights, report AMI-296, January 2020, https://www.absolutemarketsinsights.com/request_sample.php?id=296.

5. See also L. Wu, B. Lou, and L. Hitt, "Data Analytics Supports Decentralized Innovation," *Management Science* 65, no. 10 (2019): 4863–4877; C. Kakatkar, V. Bilgram, and J. Füller, "Innovation Analytics: Leveraging Artificial Intelligence in the Innovation Process," *Business Horizons* 63, no. 2 (2020): 171–181.

6. M. Mariani and S. Nambisan, *Innovation Analytics and Digital Innovation Experimentation: The Rise of Research-Driven Online Review Platforms* (working paper, 2021).

7. S. Nambisan and M. Sawhney, "A Buyer's Guide to the Innovation Bazaar," *Harvard Business Review* 85, no. 6 (2007): 109.

8. For more on open innovation as a directed activity, see T. Felin and T. R. Zenger, "Open Innovation: A Theory-Based View," *Strategic Management Review* 1 (2020): 223–232.

9. This account is based on S. Nambisan's interaction with a senior executive in the company who did not want to divulge the company's identity.

10. For example, see R. M. Holmes Jr., H. Li, M. A. Hitt, K. DeGhetto, and T. Sutton, "The Effects of Location and MNC Attributes on MNCs' Establishment of Foreign R&D Centers: Evidence from China," *Long Range Planning* 49, no. 5 (2016): 594–613.

11. Although the employees of the hub firms have to sign a confidentiality agreement with AstraZeneca (because they can come across classified information), they enjoy the same access to all facilities as the company's own employees do. For more on this, read W. B. Kemneland and A. Styhre, "Corporate Hub as a Governance Structure for Coupled Open Innovation in Large Firms," *Creativity and Innovation Management* 28, no. 4 (2019): 450–463.

12. For more on the role of digital technologies in such accelerators and entrepreneurial ecosystems, read *Beyond Borders: Digitizing Entrepreneurship for Impact* (Geneva: World Economic Forum, September 2019), http://www3.weforum .org/docs/WEF_Digitizing_Entrepreneurship_for_Impact_Report.pdf. Also visit the Startup Commons website at https://www.startupcommons.org/.

13. P. Sawers, "Startup Accelerators Forge Ahead with New Virtual Programs," VentureBeat, April 1, 2020, https://venturebeat.com/2020/04/01/startup-accelerators -forge-ahead-with-new-virtual-programs/.

14. "Smart Home," Statista, accessed March 22, 2021, https://www.statista.com /outlook/283/100/smart-home/worldwide.

15. *2020 Digital Trends: Deep Dive: Putting the Customer in Context* (Econsultancy and Adobe, 2019), industry report, https://www.adobe.com/content/dam /www/us/en/offer/digital-trends-2020/digital-trends-2020-marketing-in-2020 .pdf.

16. *Digital Asset Management Market: Global Industry Trends, Share, Size, Growth, Opportunity and Forecast 2020-2025*, Research and Markets, March 2020, https:// www.researchandmarkets.com/reports/5009108/digital-asset-management -market-global-industry?utm_source=dynamic&utm_medium=GNOM&utm _code=q2rpnp&utm_campaign=1375916+-+Digital+Asset+Management+Indus try+Worth+%248.5+Billion+by+2025+-+Rising+Demand+for+Workflow+Colla

boration+%26+Automation%2c+Cloud-based+DAM+Solutions+Offer+Improve
d+Access+to+Digital+Assets&utm_exec=joca220gnomd.

17. M. L. Weitzman, "Recombinant Growth," *Quarterly Journal of Economics* 113, no. 2 (1998): 331–360.

18. The write-up on Johnson Controls' digital innovation initiative is based partly on S. Nambisan's interview with Samuel Freeman, the company's former global innovation director.

19. "Johnson Controls Launches OpenBlue," Cision PR Newswire, July 31, 2020, https://www.prnewswire.com/news-releases/johnson-controls-launches -openblue-301103666.html.

20. P. High, "Assembling the Largest Intelligent Building Company in the World," *Forbes*, April 13, 2020; https://www.forbes.com/sites/peterhigh/2020/04 /13/assembling-the-largest-intelligent-building-company-in-the-world/#70eacd 7e33d5.

21. Based on an interview with S. Nambisan.

Chapter 7

1. For the conventional view, see J. Johanson and J.-E. Vahlne, "The Internationalization Process of the Firm—A Model of Knowledge Development and Increasing Foreign Market Commitments," *Journal of International Business Studies* 8 (1977): 23–32. For new perspectives on internationalization processes, see M. P. Koza, S. Tallman, and A. Ataay, "The Strategic Assembly of Global Firms," *Global Strategy Journal* 1 (2011): 27–46; S. Tallman, Y. Luo, and P. Buckley, "Business Models in Global Competition," *Global Strategy Journal* 8, no. 4 (2018): 517–535.

2. See Y. Luo and R. Tung, "A General Theory of Springboard MNEs," *Journal of International Business Studies* 49, no. 2 (2018): 129–152; Y. Luo and R. Tung, "International Expansion of Emerging Market Enterprises: A Springboard Perspective," *Journal of International Business Studies* 38, no. 4 (2007): 481–498.

3. For more on business models in a general setting, see C. Zott and R. Amit, "Business Model Design and the Performance of Entrepreneurial Firms," *Organization Science* 18, no. 2 (2007): 181–199; R. Amit and C. Zott, "Creating Value through Business Model Innovation," *Sloan Management Review* 53, no. 3 (2012): 41–49; M. W. Johnson, C. M. Christensen, and H. Kagermann, "Reinventing Your Business Model," *Harvard Business Review* 86, no. 12 (2008):

50–59; H. Chesbrough, *Open Business Models: How to Thrive in the New Innovation Landscape* (Brighton, MA: Harvard Business School Press, 2006).

4. "Bayer CropScience Ties Up with ITC's Agri Business," Money Control, June 15, 2020, https://www.moneycontrol.com/news/business/bayer-cropscience-ties -up-with-itcs-agri-business-5407871.html.

Chapter 8

1. In June 2020, Nabbesh was acquired by Dubai-based freelance marketplace Ureed.

2. N. Bosma, S. Hill, A. Ionescu-Somers, D. Kelley, J. Levie, and G. A. Tarnawa. *Global Entrepreneurship Monitor 2019/2020 Global Report* (London: Global Entrepreneurship Research Association, 2020), https://www.gemconsortium.org/file /open?fileId=50443.

3. J. Manyika et al., *Digital Globalization*.

4. See S. Nambisan, "Digital Entrepreneurship: Toward a Digital Technology Perspective of Entrepreneurship," *Entrepreneurship Theory and Practice* 41, no. 6 (2017): 1029–1055.

5. For example, read H. Aldrich, "The Democratization of Entrepreneurship? Hackers, Makerspaces, and Crowdfunding" (paper presented at the annual meeting of the Academy of Management, Philadelphia, PA, August 1–5, 2014); A. Pergelova, T. Manolova, R. Simeonova-Ganeva, and D. Yordanova, "Democratizing Entrepreneurship? Digital Technologies and the Internationalization of Female-Led SMEs," *Journal of Small Business Management* 57, no. 1 (2019): 14–39.

6. E. Autio, S. Nambisan, L. D. Thomas, and M. Wright, "Digital Affordances, Spatial Affordances, and the Genesis of Entrepreneurial Ecosystems," *Strategic Entrepreneurship Journal* 12, no. 1 (2018): 72–95.

7. H. Varian. "Micromultinationals Will Run the World," *Foreign Policy*, August 15, 2011, https://foreignpolicy.com/2011/08/15/micromultinationals-will-run -the-world/.

8. Interview with Y. Luo in April 2020.

9. Interview with S. Nambisan in May 2020.

10. Interview with S. Nambisan in May 2020.

11. Interview with S. Nambisan in May 2020.

12. B. Clark and B. McKenzie, "Blockchain and IP Law: A Match made in Crypto Heaven?," World Intellectual Property Organization, February 2018, https://www.wipo.int/wipo_magazine/en/2018/01/article_0005.html.

13. Post-COVID-19, SoftBank and other venture capital firms have drawn down some of their support for several digital-born globals, including OYO.

14. For more on digital technology affordances and how it shapes entrepreneurship, read A. Majchrzak and M. L. Markus, "Technology Affordances and Constraints in Management Information Systems (MIS)," in *Encyclopedia of Management Theory*, ed. E. Kessler (Thousand Oaks, CA: SAGE Publications, 2012), 832–836; S. Nambisan, "Digital Entrepreneurship."

15. J. Suk-yee, "Lawmakers to Deliberate Bills on Global IT Firms' Free-Riding of Korean Telecom Networks," *BusinessKorea*, May 6, 2020, http://www.businesskorea.co.kr/news/articleView.html?idxno=45296.

16. Interview with S. Nambisan in June 2020.

Chapter 9

1. Y. Luo, "Political Risk and Country Risk in International Business: Concepts and Measures," in *The Oxford Handbook of International Business*, 2nd ed. ed. A.M. Rugman (Oxford: Oxford University Press, 2009).

2. E. Braw, "Chinese Acquisitions of Western Firms Threaten National Security," *Foreign Policy*, August 24, 2020, https://foreignpolicy.com/2020/08/24/chinese-acquisitions-of-western-firms-threaten-national-security/.

3. K. Benner and N. Perlroth, "China-Backed Hackers Broke into 100 Firms and Agencies, U.S. Says," *New York Times*, September 16, 2020, https://www.nytimes.com/2020/09/16/us/politics/china-hackers.html.

4. M. Singh, "The 2007–2008 Financial Crisis in Review," Investopedia, updated Jan 11, 2021, https://www.investopedia.com/articles/economics/09/financial-crisis-review.asp.

5. "Biggest Cyber Attacks and Their Cost for the Global Economy," Technology.org, July 17, 2019, https://www.technology.org/2019/07/17/biggest-cyber-attacks-and-their-cost-for-the-global-economy/.

6. E. Braw, "Is Hacking an 'Act of War'?," *Wall Street Journal*, August 21, 2019, https://www.wsj.com/articles/is-hacking-an-act-of-war-11566428091?mod=searchresults&page=1&pos=4. See also S. Pinker, "When Taking Risks Is the Best

Strategy," *Wall Street Journal*, August 21, 2019, https://www.wsj.com/articles /when-taking-risks-is-the-best-strategy-11566401041?mod=searchresults&page =1&pos=1.

7. J. Harpaz, "Public Shaming of Big Companies Not as Big a Deal, but Not Going Away Anytime Soon," *Forbes*, June 26, 2017, https://www.forbes.com /sites/joeharpaz/2017/06/26/public-shaming-of-big-companies-not-as-big-a -deal-as-youd-think-but-not-going-away-anytime-soon/#5291170f6333.

8. S. Gaultier-Gaillard and J.-P. Louisot, "Risks to Reputation: A Global Approach," *Geneva Papers on Risk and Insurance* 31, no. 3 (2006): 425–445.

9. B. Chakravorti and R. Chaturvedi, "Which Countries Were (and Weren't) Ready for Remote Work," *Harvard Business Review*, April 29, 2020, https://hbr .org/2020/04/which-countries-were-and-werent-ready-for-remote-work?.

10. Wikipedia contributors, "Global Connectivity Index," Wikipedia, updated November 12, 2020, https://en.wikipedia.org/wiki/Global_Connectivity_Index. See also "Methodology," Global Connectivity Index, accessed March 22, 2021, https://www.huawei.com/minisite/gci/en/methodology.html.

11. J. Boillet, "Why AI Is Both a Risk and a Way to Manage Risk," EY, April 1, 2018, https://www.ey.com/en_gl/assurance/why-ai-is-both-a-risk-and-a-way-to -manage-risk.

12. See https://www.digitalindia.gov.in/.

13. "E-Commerce: India," Statista, accessed March 22, 2021, https://www .statista.com/outlook/243/119/ecommerce/india.

14. P. Michelman, "Leading to Become Obsolete," *MIT Sloan Management Review*, June 19, 2017, https://sloanreview.mit.edu/article/leading-to-become-obsolete/.

Chapter 10

1. For more on the challenges related to the concept of working from anywhere, read P. Choudhury, "Our Work-from-Anywhere Future," *Harvard Business Review*, November 2020, https://hbr.org/2020/11/our-work-from-anywhere-future.

2. E. Dane and B. J. Brummel, "Examining Workplace Mindfulness and Its Relations to Job Performance and Turnover Intention." *Human Relations* 67, no. 1 (2014): 105–128; P. K. Hyland, R. A. Lee, and M. J. Mills, "Mindfulness at Work: A New Approach to Improving Individual and Organizational Performance," *Industrial and Organizational Psychology* 8, no. 4 (2015): 576; D. J. Good, C. J.

Lyddy, T. M. Glomb, J. E. Bono, K. W. Brown, M. K. Duffy, R. A. Baer, J. A. Brewer, and S. W. Lazar, "Contemplating Mindfulness at Work: An Integrative Review," *Journal of Management* 42, no. 1 (2016): 114–142.

3. B. H. Gunaratana, *Mindfulness in Plain English* (Boston: Wisdom Publications, 2011).

4. Interview with S. Nambisan in June 2020.

5. J.-P. Martini, "Unleashing the Power of Mindfulness in Corporations," BCG, April 26, 2018, https://www.bcg.com/publications/2018/unleashing-power-of -mindfulness-in-corporations.aspx. See also K. Schaufenbuel, "Why Google, Target and General Mills Are Investing in Mindfulness," *Harvard Business Review*, December 28, 2015, https://hbr.org/2015/12/why-google-target-and-general-mills-are -investing-in-mindfulness.

6. An alternate conceptualization of digital intelligence (offered by Forrester Research), situated in the context of digital marketing, equates it to the insights gained from the analysis of customer data to optimize customer experiences. See J. McCormick and C. Little, *Optimize Customer Experiences with Digital Intelligence* (Forrester, February 23, 2016). Digital intelligence has also been viewed as a new type of human capacity that brings together skills and capabilities related to the use of digital technologies in people's private and professional lives.

7. P. High, "Assembling the Largest Intelligent Building Company in the World," *Forbes*, April 13, 2020, https://www.forbes.com/sites/peterhigh/2020/04/13 /assembling-the-largest-intelligent-building-company-in-the-world.

8. For example, see J. Birkinshaw, "The New Boardroom Imperative: From Agility to Resilience," *Forbes*, March 28, 2020, https://www.forbes.com/sites /lbsbusinessstrategyreview/2020/03/28/the-new-boardroom-imperative-from -agility-to-resilience/; D. Simchi-Levi and E. Simchi-Levi, "Building Resilient Supply Chains Won't Be Easy," *Harvard Business Review*, June 23, 2020, https:// hbr.org/2020/06/building-resilient-supply-chains-wont-be-easy; K. Alicke, E. Barrriball, S. Lund, and D. Swan, "Is Your Supply Chain Risk Blind—or Risk Resilient?," McKinsey & Company, May 14, 2020, https://www.mckinsey.com /business-functions/operations/our-insights/is-your-supply-chain-risk-blind-or -risk-resilient#.

9. There is a rich stream of research on organizational resilience. For recent reviews of this research, see T. A. Williams, D. A. Gruber, K. M. Sutcliffe, D. A. Shepherd, and E. Y. Zhao, "Organizational Response to Adversity: Fusing

Crisis Management and Resilience Research Streams," *Academy of Management Annals* 11, no. 2 (2017): 733–769; M. K. Linnenluecke, "Resilience in Business and Management Research: A Review of Influential Publications and a Research Agenda," *International Journal of Management Reviews* 19 (2017): 4–30; S. Duchek, "Organizational Resilience: A Capability-Based Conceptualization," *Business Research* 13 (2020): 215–246; C. A. Lengnick-Hall, T. E. Beck, and M. L. Lengnick-Hall, "Developing a Capacity for Organizational Resilience through Strategic Human Resource Management," *Human Resource Management Review* 21, no. 3 (2011): 243–255.

10. For more on such a processual view of organizational resilience, see S. Duchek, "Organizational Resilience."

11. For example, see J. M. Kaplan, T. Bailey, D. O'Halloran, A. Marcus, and C. Rezek, *Beyond Cybersecurity: Protecting Your Digital Business* (Hoboken, NJ: John Wiley & Sons, 2015).

12. Interview with S. Nambisan in May 2020.

Index

Page numbers followed by t refer to tables.

Organisation for Economic Co-
operation and Development
(OECD), 169
OYO, 2–4, 98, 148, 212n13

Panama Canal, 1
Panasonic, 170
Path dependence, 46, 132
PayPal, 146
Paytm Mall, 59
Personally Controlled Electronic
Health Record, 34, 39
Personal protective equipment (PPE),
98
Philip Morris International (PMI),
105–107, 184
Philippines, 148
Philips Healthcare, 3, 85–87, 161,
206n13
Phoenix Children's Hospital, 85
Pinduoduo, 14, 55
Pinkberry, 64
Pizza Hut, 43
Platform-market connectivity, 44t,
74–83, 177t
Platforms
Alibaba, 9, 14, 60, 74, 86, 142,
144
analytics and, 80, 86
Android, 29, 59, 82
Apple, 34
artificial intelligence (AI) and, 80–
81, 86
ARTIK Smart IoT, 86
Bayer, 81–83, 86–87
business models and, 131, 134–138
China and, 34, 58, 74, 76, 86–87,
89, 97–98, 103
Climate FieldView, 81–83, 117

cloud computing, 9, 15, 23, 85–86,
122, 125, 136, 142, 156, 162, 166–
167, 170, 172
competition and, 71
consumers and, 73–74, 85
coupling and, 74–77, 83–84, 87–88
data value and, 73
Demandware, 134
digital assets and, 29, 44, 65, 71–88,
109, 117, 121, 125
digital embrace strategy and, 83–88,
177t
digital global business connectivity
and, 28–34, 38, 43–44
digital handshake strategy and, 83–
84, 87–88, 177t
digitization and, 3–4, 7–15, 22–23
distinctiveness and, 75, 79, 81, 83,
87
e-Choupal 4.0, 136
ecosystems and, 72–75, 82–89
efficiency and, 78–81
entrepreneurship and, 141–147,
152–153
European Union (EU) and, 5, 33–34,
76, 79, 81–82, 87
foreign subsidiaries and, 73, 89, 104,
109–121, 125
global platform strategy and, 74–83,
88, 144–147, 177t
Google, 28
HealthSuite, 3, 85–86, 206n13
India and, 74, 79–83, 86–87
innovation and, 83–86
Internet of Things (IoT), 86, 89
less influence of, 73
localization and, 72–83, 86–89
markets and, 44t, 50–51, 57–70,
74–83, 177t